Writing Warm Ups

70 Activities for Prewriting

Abigail Tom
St. Louis University

Heather McKay

ALEMANY PRESS
REGENTS/PRENTICE HALL
Englewood Cliffs, New Jersey 07632

Acknowledgements

Some of the activities in this book appear in other sources in another form. We are grateful to the following for guidance and inspiration with regard to the indicated activities:

Braun, Dorit and Jean Pearson. *Priorities for Development*. Development Education Center, Selly Oak Colleges, Birmingham, England, 1981. (pp. 37–38, Map Views)

Byrne, Donn and Shelagh Rixon. *ELT 1 Guide 1: Communication Games*. NFER-Nelson, Windsor, England, 1979. (p. 62, We're Related; p. 64 Grids)

The Puzzle Book. Childcraft Annual, World Book Inc., Chicago, 1982. (p. 90, Riddles)

Editor: Helen Munch
Copy Editor: Marc Lecard, Capp Street Editorial

Production/Design: Carol Gee
Cover: Carol Gee
Compositor: Arlene Hardwick, Elizabeth Tong

A Simon & Schuster Company
Englewood Cliffs, New Jersey 07632

Printed in the United States of America
10 9 8 7 6 5 4 3 2 1

ISBN 0-13-971110-4

Prentice-Hall International (UK) Limited, *London*
Prentice-Hall of Australia Pty. Limited, *Sydney*
Prentice-Hall Canada Inc., *Toronto*
Prentice-Hall Hispanoamericana, S. A., *Mexico*
Prentice-Hall of India Private Limited, *New Delhi*
Prentice-Hall of Japan, Inc., *Tokyo*
Simon & Schuster Asia Pte. Ltd., *Singapore*
Editora Prentice-Hall do Brasil, Ltda., *Rio de Janeiro*

Contents

*These activities have corresponding duplicatable student exercise sheets. Consult the appropriate *Notes to the Teacher* for the correct page references.

Key to activity levels:

LI = Low intermediate HI = high intermediate
I = intermediate V = variable

ORGANIZING ACTIVITIES

*These activities have corresponding duplicatable student exercise sheets. Consult the appropriate *Notes to the Teacher* for the correct page references.

Key to activity levels:

LI = Low intermediate   HI = high intermediate
I = intermediate   V = variable

Introduction

Why We Wrote This Book

Writing Warm Ups grew out of several personal teaching concerns. The first was the need for stimulating prewriting activities to support, supplement, or supplant work done in the students' core writing text. *Writing Warm Ups* offers 70 such activities that add interest and an element of surprise to the regular classroom lesson.

The second concern was the need for writing materials that can be used in a variety of teaching situations with students of different language proficiencies. The activities in *Writing Warm Ups* are appropriate for high school, adult school, and university students with low to high intermediate English proficiency. In addition, many of the activities can be adapted for use with students at various proficiency levels.

The third concern was that the materials be ready for use with minimal preparation and/or apparatus required. All of the activities in *Writing Warm Ups* provide easy-to-follow teacher notes and most of the activities feature duplicatable student exercise sheets with directions to the teacher or students. An occasional activity may call for the use of an overhead projector or a tape recorder; however, the majority of activities require no more than large sheets of paper (newsprint), markers, tape, and/or copies of a duplicatable exercise sheet.

A final concern was the need for materials that are both intellectually challenging and linguistically suitable for the ages and proficiency levels of the students. Many activities in *Writing Warm Ups* provide students with sophisticated intellectual tasks while controlling the level of linguistic input and output. Many are designed to tap each student's knowledge, background, and experience.

About This Book

Writing Warm Ups is a resource book of 70 activities for teachers of writing to students whose native language is not English. The activities are *prewriting* activities. That is, they are intended to be introduced before any extended writing is done, to sensitize students to the decisions they must make while writing, and to familiarize them with the options available to them in writing. In this way, students practice making decisions and selecting options, and achieve an understanding of the writing process without having to worry about "getting the words down" on paper. The activities require students to combine several language skills while exploring the concepts that underlie writing.

How This Book Is Organized

Writing Warm Ups consists of eight units divided into two parts. The first part, Focusing Activities, covers the sociolinguistic aspects of writing in four units: Audience, Purpose, Point of View, and Focus. The second part, Organizing Activities, deals with the ways in which ideas within a text may be related, in four more units: Classification, Sequence, Cause and Effect, and Comparison and Contrast. The units and the activities within each unit are arranged according to perceived level of conceptual difficulty. A minimum level of English proficiency is suggested for each activity. However, because the underlying concepts are challenging to all students, the activities may be used by students with a higher proficiency level than the one indicated.

Each *Writing Warm Ups* unit begins with an introduction and Notes to the Teacher for the activities in that unit. The notes indicate the time, organization, level, and materials required for the activity as well as activity directions and suggestions for variations and follow-up. A list of composition topics designed to help students apply each unit's concepts follows the notes. Each unit concludes with the duplicatable student exercise sheets for particular activities in that unit. An Answer Key at the end of the book provides answers for selected activities with exercise sheets.

How to Use This Book

The first step in using *Writing Warm Ups* is to select a unit that corresponds to classroom work in progress and an activity that is appropriate for the students' level. Check the Contents (pp. iii–iv) for a list of the activities and the minimum proficiency level for each. The Contents also indicates whether or not an activity has a duplicatable exercise sheet. Next, read the Notes to the Teacher for the activity you have chosen. Note the length of time, class organization (whole class, small groups, pairs), and the materials required for the activity. In most cases, the activity directions assume at the outset that the class has been arranged according to the indicated Organization. If an activity has an exercise sheet, check the directions on the sheet to see how many copies are needed. In some activities, students working in small groups or in pairs share one exercise sheet to ensure cooperation rather than independent work.

Following an activity, be sure to check the Answer Key if specific answers are expected. However, be aware that for many activities there are no "right" or "wrong" answers. Answers may vary according to the cultural backgrounds and experiences of the students.

A Final Note

Some of the activities in *Writing Warm Ups* may be adaptations of activities that appear in other publications. Whenever possible, we have cited those activities and publications in the *Acknowledgements* (p. ii).

We hope that you find *Writing Warm Ups* helpful in your teaching and that you and your students enjoy using it with good results.

Abigail Tom
Heather McKay

Focusing Activities

Unit 1 Audience

Notes to the Teacher

Introduction

Every time we communicate with anyone in any way, we have an audience. In order to communicate effectively with that audience, we must consider carefully the *register* and *content* of the message.

Register

Register, the manner in which we communicate, is largely determined by the circumstances and social relationships surrounding the communication. In speaking, because we are face to face with our audience, we can adjust our form of address, body language, vocabulary, and even accent, to our audience. When we write, we cannot see our audience; indeed, in many cases we do not even know exactly who it will be. Although we make fewer distinctions about register when writing, we clearly differentiate between formal and informal writing. A student who submits a slang-filled essay will be criticized for writing too informally. Likewise, we would not begin a letter to our parents, "Gentlemen: In regard to your letter of the 20th . . ."

Content

In addition to varying the register of our message according to our audience, we must also vary its content according to the information we can assume our audience already possesses. When communicating with family and friends, we may refer to people and places without further explanation because we share a common background. Similarly, when we write notes to ourselves, we need only jot down a few words as reminders of the whole message. In contrast, we could scarcely communicate with a stranger if our messages only consisted of such fragments of information. Our audience would lack the information needed to fill in the missing connections. When we communicate across cultures, there are even more missing connections. People, places, or events that are well known to the people of one country may be unfamiliar to those of another. Underlying political or religious assumptions may not be shared or may be misunderstood. Because the audience for much formal writing is not present, the author must make predictions about the information the reader will bring to it. Thus, a writer can assume that people who read scholarly linguistics journals have a background in that field, that those who read student newspapers are connected with the academic community in some way, and so forth.

Unit 1 The purpose of this unit is to make students aware of their audiences. Students will both identify intended audiences and construct messages for different audiences, taking into account both the register and content of their messages.

What I Write

Time:	10–15 minutes
Organization:	whole class or small groups
Level:	intermediate
Materials:	*exercise sheet, p. 11*

Ask students to tell you about the different kinds of writing they do in English and in their native languages. Some examples are class notes, lists, assignments, diary or journal entries, papers, letters, personal notes, messages, poems, or stories. Distribute copies of the exercise sheet, one per student. Review the directions and answer any questions. You might want to give an example to get students started.

If the class is large, students can work in small groups to fill in the charts. Groups can then compare charts and discuss any differences. When students have completed their exercise sheets, ask them to think about how they write for different audiences and to explain how their writing may differ from audience to audience.

Reactions

Time:	10–15 minutes
Organization:	pairs and small groups (4, then 8 students)
Level:	low intermediate
Materials:	a poster or picture of something that evokes a strong reaction (an abstract painting, a sculpture, an animal)

Show the picture to the class and ask students to write down briefly their reactions to it. Have students compare their answers, first in pairs, next in groups of four, and, if you wish, in groups of eight. Then ask each group to share its ideas with the entire class. Explain to the class that there are "no right answers" and that the purpose of the activity is to illustrate how people react differently to the same stimulus depending on their background and experience.

Other media or stimuli can be used, such as poems or short silent films in which the message is not explicit. Some films we have found at the public library are: *Urbanissimo, A Chairy Tale, Autobiography of* *, and various short Marcel Marceau films.

Who's It For?

Time: 20–30 minutes
Organization: small groups (3–4 students)
Level: variable
Materials: a variety of magazine advertisements for each group (ads should be appropriate for the audiences noted on the exercise sheet); *exercise sheet, p. 12.*

Distribute the advertisements and copies of the exercise sheet to each group, one per student. Review the directions and answer any questions. Provide an example if necessary. Explain that any disagreements about placement of items on the chart should be discussed until a consensus is reached.

As a variation, use videotapes of TV commercials (for a whole-class activity) or personal ads from magazines or newspapers. (The latter require more extensive knowledge of English and of American culture.) Other audiences can be featured on the chart, too, such as Urban/Rural, Age Groups (3–10, 10–20, 20–30, and so on), or Single/Married.

As a follow-up, have students write their own ads for an item they want to sell. Students must take into account the kind of person who might want to buy the item.

Audience, Audience

Time: 10–20 minutes
Organization: small groups (3–4 students)
Level: high intermediate
Materials: *exercise sheet, p. 13*

Distribute copies of the exercise sheet, one per student. Review the directions and answer any questions. When students have completed the exercise sheet, have each group think of and write down two or three topics that would be of interest to each of the audiences listed. For example, "tracking bears" would interest hunters.

As a variation, use newspaper comic strips with clearly identifiable audiences ("Donald Duck," "Doonesbury," "Sally Forth," "Cathy"). Beware of inherent cultural and linguistic difficulties, however. Or try using school and community calendar announcements, having students identify who would be interested in a particular event.

Advertisements

Time:	15–20 minutes
Organization:	groups (5–6 students)
Level:	low intermediate
Materials:	a variety of magazine advertisements for each group (ads should be appropriate for the audiences named on the exercise sheet); *exercise sheet, p. 14,* envelope for holding the audience strips

Distribute the advertisements to each group and give one audience strip to each student (see exercise sheet). Tell students to keep the information on their audience strips a secret. Ask each student to select the ad or ads that would appeal most to the audience listed on the strip. Then have the other group members guess who the audience is for each ad. The same ad may appeal to more than one audience.

Match This!

Time:	15–20 minutes
Organization:	whole class
Level:	low intermediate
Materials:	*exercise sheet, p. 15*; envelope for holding dialog strips

Distribute the dialog strips one per student (see exercise sheet). Instruct students to walk around the room until they find a matching dialog strip. If the class is large, divide it in half or thirds to make the activity more manageable. When each student has found a matching strip, have the resulting student pairs read their dialogs to the rest of the class. Students will judge whether or not the dialog strips are correctly matched and whether the dialogs are appropriate in terms of their formality or informality.

As a variation, try using other functions such as complaints, promises, and threats, but don't mix functions.

Role Play

Time: 30–45 minutes
Organization: small groups (4 students)
Level: high intermediate
Materials: *exercise sheet, p. 16*; envelope for holding role play cards

Divide the class into four groups (eight groups if class is large). Distribute the role cards so that all members of the same group have the same card (see exercise sheet). In addition, give a grade report card to the "student" and the "counselor" groups. Allow 5-10 minutes for students to study and discuss their roles. Then regroup the students so that all four roles are represented in each group. Read the following situation to the students:

X is a high school student. His school sent his grade report to his parents, but **X** got it first. Meanwhile, the school counselor called **X**'s parents to arrange an immediate appointment to discuss **X**'s academic problems.

Explain to the class that each student will assume the role indicated on his or her role card. Students will simultaneously discuss the problem with other group members in the following order:

Step 1: counselor and parent, student and friend;
Step 2: parent and student, counselor and friend;
Step 3: student and counselor, parent and friend;
Step 4: all four discuss possible solutions.

Be sure to move on to the next step as soon as any member of the class appears tired of a given step, usually within 5–10 minutes. When all groups have completed Step 4, discuss together the various group solutions.

The Parking Problem

Time: 1 hour plus
Organization: small groups (2 or 3 students)
Level: high intermediate
Materials: *exercise sheets, pp. 17–18*

This is a particularly good activity for a class in which students work at differing paces. Students can be paired or grouped with others who work at a similar pace. All groups need not cover all of the exercise sheets.

Explain to the class that each group is to play the part of George Nelson, a high school assistant principal. Distribute copies of the first exercise sheet (p. 17), one per student, and read the story aloud or have students read silently. Answer any questions. Then read the memo to "George" (p. 17) and ask students to respond to it in writing. As students complete their responses, collect the papers and hand out the next exercise sheet (p. 18). Let each group work at its own pace, responding to one exercise sheet before going on to the next.

As a follow-up, read (or ask students to read) individual responses to The Parking Problem and discuss possible solutions.

Composition Topics

1. Describe to a foreigner an event in the history of your country.
2. Describe a familiar place to a person who has never been there.
3. Write two short letters about a bad experience you had. Write one to your parents and one to your best friend.
4. Write an evaluation of one of your classes (or teachers) for your teacher to read.
5. Write a composition about a problem in your country. Before you begin, think about how you would write it for different audiences (for example, people in the United States, people in your country, people in a neighboring country). Decide which audience you are addressing before starting to write.
6. Explain some aspect of your culture, such as religion, to a person who knows nothing about it.
7. Write about a place that is special to you. First choose your audience. It could be a tourist, an artist, a historian, an older person, a child, and so on.
8. Explain something about a class you are taking so that a person who doesn't know anything about the subject can understand it.

What I Write

Directions: Think about the different kinds of writing you do (letters, notes, lists). Then identify the audiences for whom you write and complete the chart below.

Myself	Friends	Teachers	Family	People I Don't Know

Who's It For?

Directions: Your teacher will give you some magazine advertisements. With your group, identify the product in the ad and the audience for whom it is intended.

Product	Families	Men	Women	Children	Retired People

Audience, Audience

Directions: With your group, read each statement below and match it with an appropriate audience.

Statement	Audience
1. "If you want to be a good language learner, it is important that you learn from your mistakes."	a. car buyers
2. "Once upon a time there was a beautiful princess who lived in a castle far away."	b. children
3. "This four-year program combines a traditional liberal arts degree with strong preparation for a career in business or industry. The student majors in a liberal arts discipline while taking selected coursework in business."	c. job applicants
4. "Each of us hunts three or four miles from our base camp, so it is essential that we have good trails with no fallen trees, logs, washouts or other obstacles."	d. foreign language students
5. "The SE Coupe comes fully equipped with a long list of comfort and convenience standards included in its price."	e. hunters
6. "Please type or print clearly on this application. You must include your social security number and the date you can begin working."	f. prospective university students

Advertisements

Directions to the teacher: Duplicate this exercise sheet and cut along the dotted lines so that each student receives an audience strip. Then follow the activity directions in the *Notes to the Teacher, p. 7.*

children	teenagers
adults	families
students	retired people
business people	travelers
golfers	tennis players
homeowners	educators
doctors	librarians
dog owners	cat owners
sick people	drivers
cyclists	music lovers

Match This!

Directions to the teacher: Duplicate this exercise sheet and cut along the dotted lines so that each student receives a dialog strip. Then follow the activity directions in the *Notes to the Teacher, p. 7.*

"John, I'd like you to meet my mother."

"How do you do, Mrs. Smith? I've heard so much about you from your son."

"Hi, Susie. Do you know Jane?"

"No. Hi, Jane. Nice to meet you."

"I don't believe we've met. I'm Nancy Jones."

"How do you do, Nancy? I'm Karen Martin."

"Dr. Miller, this is Allen Brown. He's here to see you about the headaches he's been having."

"How do you do, Mr. Brown? Come this way, please."

"Oh, Aunt Jane, I'd like you to meet my friend Ann. Ann, this is my aunt, Jane White."

"I'm so glad to meet you, Mrs. White. I've heard a lot about you from Mary."

"Hi, John. Good to see you. Say, have you met my roommate? This is George."

"How do you do, George? It is indeed a pleasure to make your acquaintance."

"How do you do, Jim? I'm Barbara Miller. I'll be your academic adviser."

"Hey, that's cool, Professor Miller."

"And now I would like to introduce Dr. Maria Martin, one of the country's foremost authorities on nuclear physics."

"Thank you for that flattering introduction."

"Don, you know Paula, don't you?"

"No, but I'd sure like to meet her!"

Role Play

Directions to the teacher: Duplicate this exercise sheet one copy per group, and cut along the dotted lines so that all members of a given group receive the same role play card. Make sure each "student X" and "counselor" group receives a grade report card. Then follow the activity directions in the *Notes to the Teacher, p. 8.*

Counselor

You work as a counselor at Central High School. Your job is to help students who have problems. You are concerned at the moment about **X**, a sophomore, who until recently has had excellent grades. Now he is failing everything except music and physical education. You are worried that if his grades don't improve, he will be unable to get into a good university.

Parent

You feel that you are a good parent. You have always encouraged your son in his studies. Until recently he has been willing to talk to you. Now he is silent and surly. When you ask him a question, he ignores you or becomes angry. You are worried that he may be using drugs. You think he is going around with the wrong kind of friends.

Student X

You are a sophomore at Central High School. Last year you had A's in all your classes. You are not feeling very happy at the moment. Everyone seems to expect a lot of you because you did so well last year. The only person who understands you is your girlfriend, who recently dropped out of school. Sometimes it all seems too much. You are thinking about dropping out and getting a job so you can earn some money.

Friend

You are a sophomore at Central High School. You get A's in all your classes. You plan to attend one of the top universities. Until recently you were good friends with **X**. You often used to talk about going to the same university. Now he doesn't want to talk to you anymore. You think this has something to do with his new group of friends, especially his new girlfriend. You feel hurt, but you still want to help him.

Grade Report

English 10	F	Algebra	F	Physical Education	C
World History	F	French 2	F	Music	C

The Parking Problem

Directions to the teacher: Duplicate copies of this exercise sheet and the one that follows (pp. 17–18) for each group in the class. Then follow the activity directions in the *Notes to the Teacher, p. 9*.

WALTER'S 'SIT-ON' SAVES CAR

When Mary Walter noticed that her red Honda was being towed from a space in front of the high school last Tuesday, she parked herself firmly on its trunk and refused to move.

"I'm not moving," she said. "I've paid $50 to park in the student lot, and there are never any spaces left by the time I get here. I used to park in the fire lanes but they kept giving me tickets. Today I decided to park in the principal's place and now they want to tow me."

When asked about the towing policy, George Nelson, Assistant Principal in charge of Student Affairs, stated that cars are automatically towed after receiving three tickets. "It is the only way we can deal with the problem of illegally parked cars on campus," he noted. Walter, however, alleged that she had not been notified of that rule prior to the arrival of the tow truck. "Every time I got a ticket I'd write a note explaining the situation and send it to Mr. Nelson's office," she said, "and they never said anything about towing. In any case, I don't think that they should sell parking stickers unless they have enough spaces."

A number of students joined Walter in the "sit-on" and managed to save several other cars from being towed. "I'm showing my solidarity," said Lynn Bryan, a senior. "My car got towed yesterday. I think it's time they started to be more humane about this towing business."

During Walter's sit-on, the driver of the tow truck tried to force open the door of her car. A security guard informed her that she would have to move sooner or later. After waiting for an hour for Walter to leave her car, the tow truck driver left.

From the desk of . . .
Franklin Farley, principal of the high school

George:

I think it's time we took some action on the parking problem. When I came to work today, I found a red Honda in my parking space. I also noticed a lot of other illegally parked cars. Some were even in fire lanes, which, as you know, puts us in violation of the law. Perhaps it's time we had the tow trucks back. Let me know what you decide.

Continued

The Parking Problem — *Continued*

To: George Nelson, Assistant Principal
From: Larry James, Fire Chief
Re: Campus fire inspection 3/20/8__

On our inspection of your campus we found the following fire code violations:

1. Fire lanes blocked by illegally parked cars
2. Fire door on 3rd floor did not open easily

Our inspector will return to the school on Monday, April 7 to check for compliance. Please indicate to me before that date the action you are taking to control parking in fire lanes.

B & B Towing and Road Service
253 South Main Street
Westville, USA 73324

Dear Mr. Nelson:

In response to your request of March 23, we sent our tow truck to the high school on March 24 to tow illegally parked cars. However, we met with considerable resistance from students who blocked our way and sat on the cars to prevent us from towing them. As you know, our charge is $30 per car, which is usually paid by the owner when claiming the towed car. Since in this case we were prevented from doing our job and cannot, therefore, reclaim our fees from the owners of the vehicles, we have no choice but to bill the school for our expenses. Please find enclosed a bill for $600 to cover these costs.

Sincerely,

Joe Bloggs

To: George Nelson
From: Campus Police
Re: Parking

We are uncertain about how to deal with the parking crisis. Ticketing has proved ineffective. We have tried tow trucks, but, as you are well aware, students became openly hostile and resisted attempts to tow their cars. What line would you like us to take next?

Unit 2 Purpose

Notes to the Teacher

Introduction

Purpose is an essential part of writing. It is impossible to write without a purpose, even if it is just to remind ourselves of something or to get our own thoughts in order. Our purpose may be varied—to inform, to persuade, to educate, to entertain—and our writing can have more than one purpose. We may seek to achieve our purpose in various ways: by appealing to humor, to the emotions, to reason, or a combination of ways. It is important for writers as well as readers to recognize the purpose of a piece of writing.

Unit 2

The following unit allows students to practice both recognizing particular purposes and attempting to achieve them.

Road Signs

Time: 10–15 minutes
Organization: small groups (3–4 students)
Level: low intermediate
Materials: *exercise sheet, p. 27*

Distribute copies of the exercise sheet, one per student. Review the directions and answer any questions. When students have completed the exercise sheet, have them think of as many signs as they can to add to each purpose category. Finally, regroup students to check and compare answers.

Sentence Strips

Time: 15 minutes
Organization: whole class
Level: low intermediate
Materials: sentence strips (see below); tape

Prior to class, prepare enough sentence strips to allow for one strip per student. Use long strips of paper and write the following sentences in letters large enough to be read from a distance:

1. Don't you think you should take an umbrella?
2. Why don't you drive more carefully?
3. Have you thought about wearing a seat belt?
4. Look out!
5. That pan is hot!
6. If you touch her, she'll bite.
7. Do you know where the coffee is?
8. Stand up straight.
9. Don't tell me you've forgotten.
10. You mustn't say that.
11. Teach your children well.
12. That's a beautiful dress you're wearing.
13. You're looking fat.
14. Where did you get that great tee shirt?
15. Where did you get that awful tee shirt?
16. That dinner was delicious.
17. Tell me when the next bus leaves, please.
18. Did you call them about the job?
19. Did you finish that book?
20. Don't forget your raincoat.

Sentence Strips — *Continued*

In class, distribute the sentence strips, one per student. Tell students to walk around the classroom looking for students whose strips share the same purpose as theirs (for example, "It's hot in here" and "Don't you ever open the window?" are both used to complain). When students have found similar strips, write the following purpose statements on the board: to ask for information, to warn, to advise, to command, to compliment, to criticize. Ask students to tape their sentence strips under a corresponding purpose statement.

With the class, discuss whether or not the purpose statements on the board match the sentence strips taped under them and whether or not some sentence strips could serve more than one purpose. Discuss the sentence strips in terms of their purpose.

Bulletin Boards

Time:	5–10 minutes the first day, 15 minutes the second day
Organization:	small groups (3–4 students)
Level:	low intermediate
Materials:	flyers, notices, and advertisements that students collect from school or neighborhood bulletin boards; tape

On the day preceding this activity talk with students about the kinds and purposes of materials they see on bulletin boards in their school or neighborhood. Together make a list of some of the purposes of such notices (to sell, to invite, to inform). Then ask students to collect as many different notices as they can from bulletin boards and to bring them to class the following day. The next day, list the purposes from the preceding day on the board. Add any new purposes to the list and divide the class into groups. Have each group arrange its notices in piles according to purpose. Then ask each group to tape the most interesting notice from each pile next to the appropriate purpose listed on the board.

As a follow-up, have each group design a flyer to persuade people to study English.

Purpose Questions

Time: 15–20 minutes
Organization: individuals, then pairs
Level: intermediate
Materials: *exercise sheet, p. 28*

Distribute copies of the exercise sheet, one per student. Review the directions and answer any questions. Look at the first question together and ask students to suggest its purpose. When students have individually finished matching questions and purpose statements, divide the class into pairs to compare answers. If pairs disagree on any answers, have one student from the pair write the disputed item(s) on the board for the whole class to discuss.

TV Programs

Time: 20–25 minutes
Organization: individuals, then small groups (3–4 students)
Level: low intermediate
Materials: *exercise sheet, p. 29*

Distribute copies of the exercise sheet, one per student. Review the directions and answer any questions. Provide an example if necessary. When students have completed the exercise sheet, divide the class into groups to compare answers. Have group members discuss any different ratings of the same TV program.

Emotions and Reason

Time:	two days, 15–20 minutes each day
Organization:	small groups (4 students)
Level:	intermediate
Materials:	pairs of advertisements from the same product category (cars, shampoo, cereals)—one advertisement that appeals to the emotions and the other to reason; extra magazines for students who forget to bring in ads; tape

Begin this activity with a discussion of advertising and its emotional and rational appeals. Consider examples of advertisements that demonstrate one appeal or the other. (Videotaped television commercials may also be used as illustrations.) Ask students to bring their own pairs of emotional/rational advertisements to the next class. The second day, divide the class into groups and have them pool all of their advertisements. Ask the groups to separate the advertisements into two categories—those with emotional appeal and those with rational appeal. Have group members discuss any disagreements. Then have each group select its most persuasive advertisement from each category and tape it onto the board. Each group will then explain its choices and the class will vote on the most persuasive ads from each category.

As a follow-up, ask students to choose something in their possession to be the subject of an advertisement. Have them consider whether to appeal to the emotions or to reason in the ad. Finally, ask students to prepare an advertisement for the object, either written or oral. If oral, it should be presented to the class and possibly videotaped.

What's Your Purpose?

Time:	15 minutes
Organization:	whole class
Level:	intermediate
Materials:	large sheets of paper; marking pens; tape

Prior to beginning this activity, discuss with students their purposes in writing. Write student responses on the board or have students write their "purpose statements" on large sheets of paper. Sample purpose statements might be:

"I write because I have to do it for my classes,"
"Writing helps me understand my own ideas," or
"I write down things I want to remember."

Tape the statements on the board or walls around the room and have students write their names next to the statements that apply to them. Next, have students indicate specific examples of their writing that illustrate their purpose statements, such as "homework—I write because I have to do it for my classes."

As a follow-up, have students write a paragraph supporting their purpose statements using the statements as their topic sentences.

Turtle Talk

Time:	20–25 minutes
Organization:	individuals, then small groups (3–4 students)
Level:	intermediate
Materials:	*exercise sheet, p. 30*

Distribute copies of the exercise sheet, one per student. Review the directions and answer any questions. Then divide the class into groups to compare answers.

As a follow-up, have students, working individually or in groups, choose another animal (an elephant, a rabbit, a bird) and create passages that illustrate two different purposes.

A Word About Smoking

Time:	15–20 minutes
Organization:	individuals, then small groups (3–4 students)
Level:	high intermediate
Materials:	*exercise sheet, p. 31*

Distribute copies of the exercise sheet, one per student. Review the directions and answer any questions. Then divide the class into small groups to compare answers and reach a consensus.

As a follow-up, have groups make up a similar list of statements for another activity such as drinking or watching TV, and to indicate the purpose of each.

Here Are the Facts

Time:	30 minutes
Organization:	small groups (3–4 students)
Level:	high intermediate
Materials:	*exercise sheet, p. 32*

Distribute copies of the exercise sheet, one per student. Review the directions and answer any questions. Explain that the "fact sheet" contains two kinds of information—one dealing with government policy, the other dealing with personal behavior. Students must first identify the kind of information each statement contains. Then they should use the information to advise the government and the people about ways to reduce crime. When all groups have determined what advice to give, regroup students and have them compare ideas.

Composition Topics

1. You want to convince your reader that your country is an excellent place to spend a vacation. Write a paragraph about a place you think tourists should visit in your country. Then think of a place you do not want to have overcrowded with tourists (your favorite beach or restaurant, for example). Write a paragraph that will discourage tourists from visiting that place.

2. Think of something that you have that nobody would want to buy (an old pair of shoes, for example). Write a paragraph advertising it for sale.

3. Think of a place you love very much. Write a paragraph about it that will make the reader share your feelings.

4. Write a story that will make your reader laugh. Then give it to a friend or classmate to read. Were you successful?

5. In most states in the United States a person can apply for a driver's license at age 16. In many other countries the minimum age is 18. Which do you think is better? Write a short composition to persuade your audience of your position.

6. You are a coach and one of your athletes wants to take an injection which will make her very strong. It will enable her to win a gold medal in the Olympics. However, if she takes it, there is a 65% chance that it will affect her brain, causing her to hear voices and have hallucinations. Persuade her either to take it or not to take it. You may appeal to her logic, her emotions or both. After you finish writing, reread your paper and write an "L" next to the statements that appeal to logic and an "E" next to those that appeal to emotion.

7. The clothing people wear communicates a message and, therefore, has a purpose. Choose one type of clothing (a conservative suit, white shirt and tie, or punk clothing, for example). Describe the clothing and the message it communicates.

8. Many traditional stories or fables such as "The Boy Who Cried Wolf" contain a moral or lesson of some kind. In one paragraph, tell such a story. Then, in another paragraph, communicate the same lesson without telling the story.

Road Signs

Directions: Look at the pictures of road signs below. On the first line beneath each picture, identify the meaning of each sign. On the second line, indicate the sign's purpose: to warn, to order, or to inform.

1. 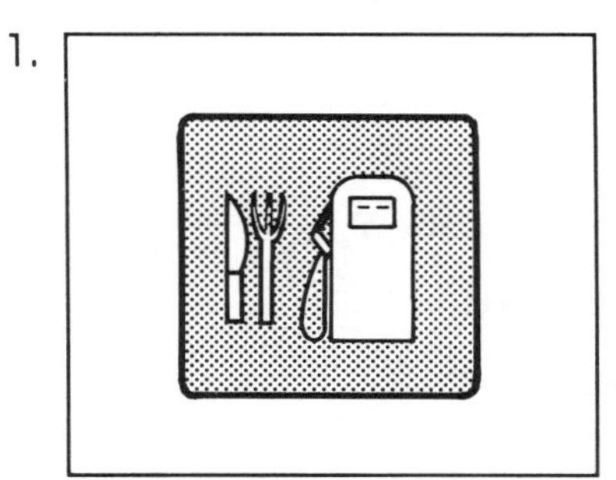

2. 

3. 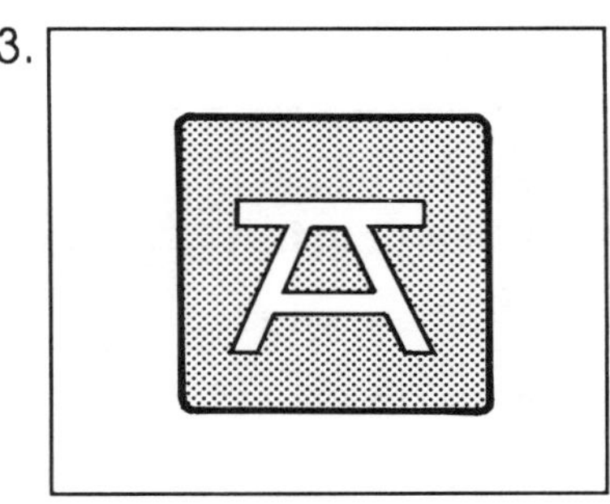

4. 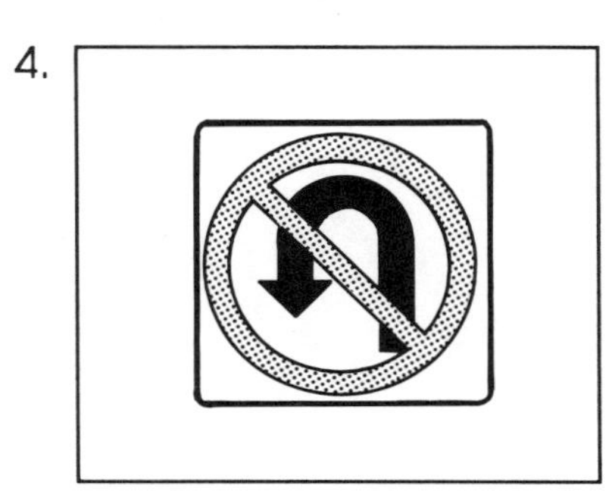

5. 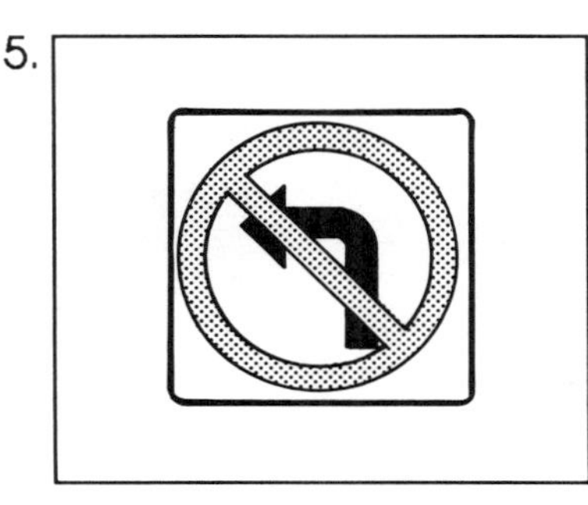

6. 

7. 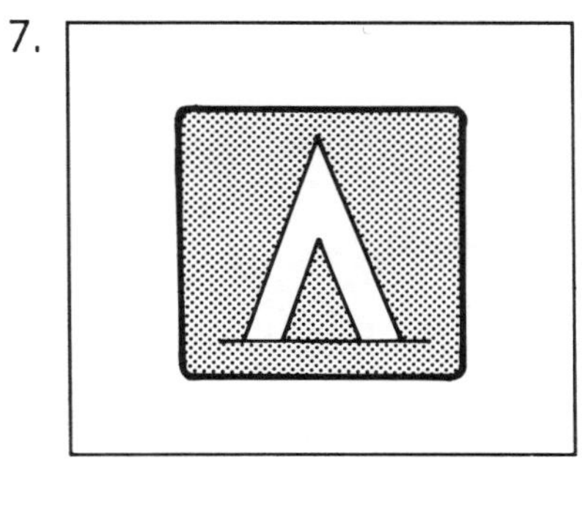

8. 

9. 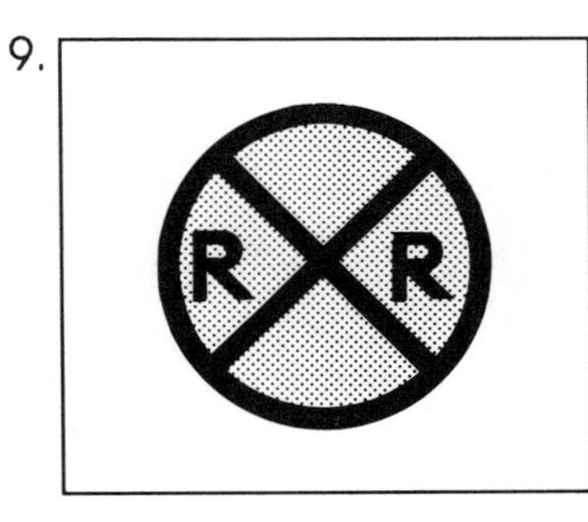

Purpose Questions

Directions: Match each question on the left to its purpose statement on the right. Some questions may have more than one purpose.

Question	Purpose Statement
1. What time is it?_______	a. to gain information
2. How are you?_______	b. to show boredom
3. Nice day, isn't it?_______	c. to be polite
4. What's the matter?_______	d. to seek agreement
5. How do you like my new car?_______	e. to seek sympathy
6. What time does the next plane leave?_______	f. to show concern
7. How's your mother getting along?_______	g. to start a conversation
8. What happened?_______	h. to seek approval
9. Do you want to talk about it?_______	
10. Did I tell you about my boyfriend?_______	
11. Did you know that my cat died?_______	
12. Did you miss the bus this morning?_______	

TV Programs

Directions: Fill in the chart below. Write the names of your favorite television programs under "Program." Then indicate what percent of each program's purpose you think is to "inform," to "persuade," to "educate," or to "entertain."

Program	To inform	To persuade	To educate	To entertain
1.				
2.				
3.				
4.				
5.				
6.				
7.				
8.				
9.				
10.				

Turtle Talk

Directions: Read each passage below and identify the writer's purpose. Then discuss your answers with your group.

1. Two turtles were having lunch together. Suddenly it started to rain. The big turtle told the small turtle, "Go home and get an umbrella." The smaller turtle said, "Only if you promise not to eat my salad." The big turtle agreed. After two years, the small turtle still hadn't come back. The big turtle decided to eat the salad. Just as he picked up his fork to taste the first bite, a voice behind him said, "If you touch that salad, I won't go get the umbrella!"

2. Turtles raised in dirty, crowded conditions may carry salmonella bacteria. Be careful when you handle pet turtles or clean their cages or equipment. Tell small children not to put their fingers in their mouths after playing with a pet turtle. Always wash your hands carefully with hot water and soap after touching the animal.

3. Throughout history people have joked about the turtle because of its shell, its walk, and its stupidity. In fact a turtle's shell is a great work of engineering and design. The two parts of the shell are joined at the sides to provide the animal with armor. This armor protects the turtle from enemies. While a turtle may not walk fast on land, it can move with amazing speed in the water. Its shape and slow walk make us think that the turtle is stupid, but that is not the case. A box turtle taken far from its home can find its way back. It seems to follow the sun or stars.

4. Once upon a time, a rabbit met a turtle. "You are very slow," the rabbit said. The turtle laughed and said, "Let's have a race, then, and see who wins." The rabbit agreed and they decided to start off at once. The turtle began to walk at his slow, steady pace. The rabbit, certain that he could win easily, decided to take a short nap before he began the race. Meanwhile the turtle continued on his slow and steady way. Suddenly the rabbit woke up and realized he had slept much longer than he had intended to. He jumped up and hopped to the finish line. He arrived just as the turtle was crossing the line. The rabbit had lost the race.

   Moral: Slow and steady wins the race.

A Word About Smoking

Directions: Read the statements and purposes below. Then indicate the purpose of each statement by writing **a**, **b**, or **c** in the blank.

Statement

_______ 1. Tobacco farming is a major source of income for many farmers.

_______ 2. Smoking helps a person relax.

_______ 3. Smoking makes a person look more mature and glamorous.

_______ 4. Smoking shortens your life.

_______ 5. Tobacco is an important agricultural export.

_______ 6. Smoking makes your teeth yellow.

_______ 7. A lot of famous people smoke.

_______ 8. Second–hand smoke is dangerous to everybody.

_______ 9. Farmers can grow tobacco on land that would not otherwise be productive.

_______ 10. Smoking gives nervous people something to do with their hands.

_______ 11. Smoking causes lung disease.

Purpose

a. To persuade people to use the product

b. To persuade people not to use the product

c. To persuade people that the product is valuable

Here Are the Facts

Directions: Read the statements about crime below. Then work with your group to decide on what advice to give to the government and to the people about crime.

1. There is more crime in societies that place a high value on individual development at the expense of family or community.[1]
2. High crime rates are correlated to high unemployment rates.[2]
3. Handguns were involved in 75% of all police killings in the United States in the 1970s and early 1980s. They have been responsible for all publicly reported assassination attempts in the United States since 1968.[3]
4. Fights that occur when guns are present are more likely to result in death than those where no guns are present.[4]
5. 80% of all violent crime is committed by people previously convicted of crimes.[5]
6. Higher penalties for crimes have not decreased the crime rate.[6]
7. You can decrease your chance of being attacked on the street by 70% if you walk with another person and by 90% if you walk with two others.[7]
8. In burglaries of more than three million American households, the burglars entered through unlocked doors or windows or used a "hidden" key.[8]

---

1. *American Violence and Public Policy*, Lyn Curtis, Ed., Yale University Press, 1985, p. 211
2. *American Violence and Public Policy*, p. 59
3. *American Violence and Public Policy*, p. 137.
4. *Thinking About Crime*, James Q. Wilson, Basic Books, Inc., New York, 1983, p. 262.
5. *Crime in America*, Ramsey Clark, Simon & Schuster, New York, 1970, p. 55
6. *American Violence and Public Policy*, p. 45
7. *Crime and Human Nature*, James Q. Wilson and Richard Hernstein, 1985, p. 73.
8. *Report to the Nation on Crime and Justice: Data*, U. S. Department of Justice, Washington, D. C. 1983, p. 31.

Unit 3 Point of View

Notes to the Teacher

Introduction

Point of view and audience are two sides of the same coin. While audience is concerned with the background and interests that the listener or reader brings to a topic, point of view concerns what the speaker or writer brings.

It is more obvious to most of us that we have an audience than that we have a point of view, since we tend to assume that there is only one point of view—our own or perhaps our society's. Many of our students have grown up in societies where there is consensus, at least in the publicly expressed point of view. Furthermore, they have attended schools in which students are not encouraged to have, or at least to express, opinions differing from the "right answer" of the textbook or the teacher. In contrast, students in schools in the United States are encouraged to express their own views, and are rewarded by teachers for doing so. Students who are inexperienced or hesitant about sharing their viewpoints are at a disadvantage in both oral and written academic work. In writing research papers, which rely on a synthesis of information, such students often have trouble recognizing the differing points of view of the sources and reconciling them to make their own point of view.

Unit 3

To make students more aware of their own viewpoints and those of others, the activities in this unit require students to examine information or situations from specific points of view; in addition, they are asked to compare differing points of view.

A Family Tree

Time: 20–30 minutes
Organization: pairs
Level: low intermediate
Materials: *exercise sheet, p. 39*

Distribute copies of the exercise sheet, one per pair. Review the directions and answer any questions. When students have completed their exercise sheets, have them compare their answers with those of other pairs.

As a follow-up, have students make their own family trees and compare them in pairs, preferably with students from different countries. Have students find differences and similarities in each other's families.

Students might also write about their families from the point of view of different family members, then exchange papers to see if they can identify which member of another student's family is speaking.

Weather Report

Time: 20–30 minutes
Organization: small groups (3–4 students)
Level: intermediate
Materials: *exercise sheet, p. 40*

Distribute copies of the exercise sheet, one per student. Review the directions and answer any questions. Then read aloud (or tape-record and play) the weather report below. Allow students to work together to complete their exercise sheets. Then have them regroup to share and compare answers.

Weather Report

"Good evening and here is the forecast for the next 24 hours. We have winter storm warnings for tonight and tomorrow. We are expecting cold temperatures tonight of 5 to 10 degrees. The winds will increase in the early evening. Snow should be moving in by late evening and will continue through tomorrow. We are expecting an accumulation of 12 to 15 inches by rush hour tomorrow morning and another 8 to 10 inches by late afternoon. Be sure to turn on your radio tomorrow morning for school closings and traffic reports."

What's the Solution?

Time:	20–30 minutes
Organization:	pairs, then whole class
Level:	high intermediate
Materials:	*exercise sheet, p. 41*

Distribute copies of one of the problems , one copy per student (see exercise sheet). Then assign a role to each student in a pair, making sure that each role is represented by an equal number of students. Ask the pairs to agree on a solution to the problem. When each pair has decided on a solution, join one pair with another pair of students representing two different roles. Ask the two pairs to find a solution that is satisfactory to both pairs. Finally, have the whole class discuss the problem and try to agree on a solution.

As a follow-up, do the remaining problem on the exercise sheet, depending on the ages and interest of your students.

Survey Someone

Time:	10–15 minutes the first day to introduce the activity; 20–30 minutes the second day to discuss responses.
Organization:	whole class, individuals, or pairs and small groups (3–4 students)
Level:	low intermediate (The survey question can be varied to suit different levels. Lower level students may feel more comfortable conducting the survey in pairs.)
Materials:	*exercise sheet, p. 42*

Distribute copies of the exercise sheet, one per student. Review the directions and answer any questions. Assign each student or pair to find three to five people to answer the survey question. Encourage students to use the question as a conversation opener.

The following day, write the question on the board and copy the exercise chart showing respondents' characteristics and the answers Yes and No. Have students record the answers they received. When all answers are on the board, ask students to generalize about the respondents who answered Yes and those who answered No. Encourage students to share their experiences as interviewers.

As a follow-up or a variation, have students prepare their own survey questions related to specific classwork.

Story Time

Time: 15–20 minutes
Organization: pairs
Level: intermediate
Materials: none

Choose a story that is familiar to the entire class. (Children's stories such as *Jack and the Beanstalk* or Aesop's fables work well.) If the students are from the same culture, any familiar folktale can be used. Alternatively, use a story the students have read in class. Review the story orally to be sure that students have the English vocabulary needed to retell it. Then divide the class into pairs. Ask each pair to retell the story from the point of view of an object or minor character in the story. Then have each pair tell their version of the story to a pair with a different point of view. Have the group of four make a list of similarities and differences in their stories. The following are suggestions for stories offering different points of view: *The Fox and the Crow* (the cheese, the tree, another crow); *The Three Billy Goats Gruff* (the bridge, the troll, a fish under the bridge); *Goldilocks* (the broken chair, the porridge, the front door); *The Three Little Pigs* (the brick house, the cauldron, the chimney); *The Boy Who Cried Wolf* (the sheep, the wolf); and *The Gingerbread Man* (the oven, the river, the farmer's wife).

Accident Report

Time: 1 hour
Organization: small groups (3–4 students)
Level: high intermediate
Materials: *exercise sheet, p. 43*

The day prior to doing this activity, distribute copies of the excercise sheet, one per student, for homework. Review the directions and answer any questions. The following day, divide the class into small groups and assign a role to each group. Ask each group to discuss the problem from the point of view of the role they have been assigned. Have the groups also discuss how they feel about the other characters. Then redivide the groups, with one representative from each of the previous groups in each new group. Ask the new groups to reach a consensus, working from the viewpoints of the roles represented. Reassemble the whole class and have group representatives explain their group's solution. Discuss the pros and cons of each one.

As a variation, select problems that reflect the interests and backgrounds of the students, or current issues.

As a follow-up, have students write short compositions indicating their opinions of the best solution.

Quotations

Time:	40 minutes
Organization:	individuals and groups (4, 8 students)
Level:	high intermediate
Materials:	*exercise sheet p. 44*

Distribute copies of the exercise sheet, one per student. Review the directions and answer any questions. When students have selected their three quotations, have them each choose a partner. The pair must discuss the quotations until they reach a consensus. Each pair must then join with another pair and again try to reach a consensus. Groups can be doubled again or groups of four can report to the whole class, giving the reasons for their choices. In place of the exercise sheets, large sheets of paper with quotations written on them can be used.

As a variation, have students produce their own comments on a given topic, individually or in small groups. The comments can be written on large sheets of paper and taped on the walls or the board. Students can sign those sheets containing comments with which they agree.

Students can also be asked to select the three quotations that they think would most likely be chosen by somebody else; for example, Americans, immigrants to the United States, people from a third country, and so on.

As a follow-up, ask some native speakers to respond to the quotations. Tape-record their comments and play five or six of the responses to the class. Have students match each response to one of the original quotations.

Map Views

Time:	15–20 minutes
Organization:	individuals, then small groups (3–4 students)
Level:	high intermediate
Materials:	*exercise sheets, pp. 45–46*

Before distributing copies of the exercise sheets, discuss the idea that maps represent a point of view. For example, a map of the world printed in the United States usually has the Americas in the middle and Asia cut into two parts. Then give each student copies of the exercise sheets showing four maps. Explain that country **X** is a small peninsular country. It shares its only land border with an unfriendly neighbor. Each of the maps has been drawn from the

Map Views — *Continued*

point of view of a different ministry. Review the directions and answer any questions. When students have completed their exercise sheets, have them work in groups to compare answers.

As a follow-up, ask students to draw a map of their own country from their individual or another person's point of view. This is a particularly interesting activity if all of the students in the class are from the same country. Students could also draw a map of the school or city from their own points of view and compare results.

Composition Topics

1. Describe your class from the point of view of a chair or a chalkboard.
2. Write a paragraph about yourself from your brother or sister's point of view. How is that different from your father's point of view?
3. Choose a film, a book or a television program that you liked and your friend did not, and write about it from your friend's point of view.
4. Describe the day you were born, from your mother or father's point of view.
5. Describe your city from the point of view of another person, such as a grandparent, a visitor, or a traffic officer.
6. People who live near a school or college have differing views of students. Describe your feelings about students from the viewpoint of *one* of the following: a neighborhood store owner, a teacher, an apartment landlord, a car dealer, a neighborhood resident, or a police officer.
7. Some people believe their parents should choose a marriage partner for them. Other people believe they should choose their partner themselves. What do you believe? Make a list of the reasons for your belief, then find a classmate who has the opposite point of view. Explain your points of view to each other. Then write a paragraph presenting your classmate's point of view. Read each other's papers to be sure that your point of view was accurately presented.
8. Two Indonesian students lived in an apartment building in the United States. One day they saw their elderly neighbor struggling upstairs with her groceries. The students rushed over to help her. One student started to pick up a bag of food. The neighbor became very angry and shouted, "I can do it myself!" The two students felt very confused. Why do you think the old woman reacted as she did? Write a paragraph giving her point of view.

A Family Tree

Directions: Look at the family tree below. Decide what the relationships are between the family members. Then, with your partner, try to identify each of the speakers of sentences 1 through 10. (There may be more than one answer in some cases.)

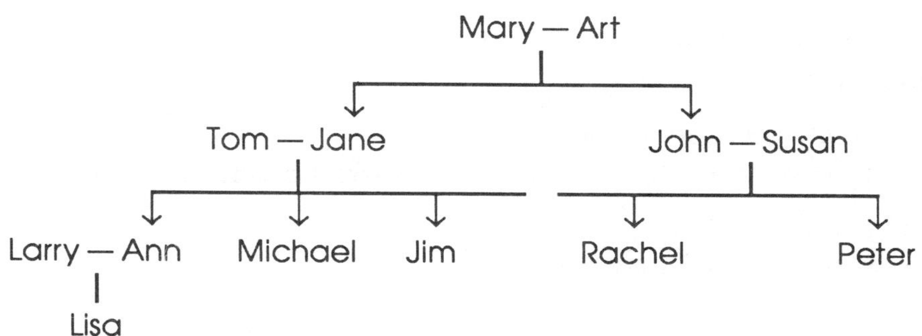

1. "I have one brother and one sister. My sister got married last year. Maybe I'll get married next year."
2. "My granddaughter got married last year to a very nice young man. My husband and I were very happy about that. Now we are even happier because they have a beautiful baby girl."
3. "My uncle's name is Tom. My sister says he's too handsome to be an uncle."
4. "My niece looks like her father, my brother. When she was a child I thought she looked more like her mother."
5. "My grandmother is named Jane. She likes to hold me and sing songs to me."
6. "I always wanted to have a brother, but my cousins are like brothers to me."
7. "My wife says that the happiest day in her life was when she married me. The happiest day in my life was when my great-granddaughter was born."
8. "My nephew Jim is 19 years old. He's my sister's younger son."
9. "My son-in-law has a good job. I wanted him to work for me, but he said that he didn't think it was a good idea to work for his father-in-law."
10. "I married John 25 years ago."

Weather Report

Directions: Read the numbered sentences below. Then listen to the weather report your teacher reads or plays on tape. Match each sentence to one of the speakers listed, **a** to **i**.

Sentence	Speaker
1. "Hey, Mom! Did you hear that? I'll bet we won't have school tomorrow!"	a. a policeman
2. "I'm so excited!! I'll finally get to see snow!! All my life I've dreamed about snow."	b. a street maintenance worker
3. "Oh, no. What am I going to do? I'm supposed to fly home tomorrow. I may not even get to the airport."	c. a child
4. "What if they don't have school tomorrow? Who is going to stay home and watch the kids? I can't take another day off from work."	d. a working mother
5. "I guess this means I'll be up all night clearing the snow off the streets. I just hope the storm doesn't last too long. The last time this happened I didn't get any sleep for three days."	e. a student from Saudi Arabia
6. "I suppose we'll really be busy tonight. People always get hurt in snowstorms, in car accidents, or just walking down the street."	f. a winter sports enthusiast
7. "How will I get to work tomorrow? I have an important appointment at 9:00 A.M. I'll never get there on time. I wish I didn't live so far from work."	g. a woman on a business trip
8. "Would you like to go skiing tomorrow? I can hardly wait to try out my new skis."	h. an emergency room nurse
9. "I can see it now. I'm going to spend all day tomorrow writing up accident reports. I wish people would learn to drive in snow."	i. a businessman who lives in the suburbs

What's the Solution?

Directions to the teacher: Select one of the problems below to present to the class. Duplicate, cut and distribute copies of this exercise sheet so that each student receives a copy of *one* of the problems. Then follow the activity directions in the *Notes to the Teacher, p. 35.*

Problem

Ann is nineteen years old. Her boyfriend, Peter, is twenty-one. Next year Ann will be a sophomore in college. She and Peter are planning to share an apartment. They feel that they are old enough to make such a decision. Neither one of them wants to get married until after they finish university. Should Ann and Peter live together before they are married?

Roles

Ann, Peter, Ann's mother, Peter's father, Ann's best friend, a religious leader whose advice Ann's parents have requested.

FOLD

Problem

Mary wants to play basketball on her school's team. She is a very good player. The coach requires all of the team members to practice after school every day. Mary's family owns a small restaurant. They expect her to work there after school and in the early evening. She cannot do both.

Roles

Mary, Mary's parents, the basketball coach, a member of the team.

Survey Someone

Directions: Find three to five people to ask the question below. Record their answers with a check (√) in the boxes below.

Question

Does watching television make people violent?

Yes	No	Male	Female	Hours watching TV less than 1	1–3	4 or more	Comment
☐	☐	☐	☐	☐	☐	☐	______
☐	☐	☐	☐	☐	☐	☐	______
☐	☐	☐	☐	☐	☐	☐	______
☐	☐	☐	☐	☐	☐	☐	______
☐	☐	☐	☐	☐	☐	☐	______

Accident Report

Directions: Read the story problem below. Then discuss it with your group from the point of view of the role your teacher has assigned you.

Problem

A factory in an Asian country had an accident. A poisonous chemical escaped into the air. The factory belonged to an important multi-national corporation. Most of the people living near the factory were poor. The poisonous chemical caused immediate breathing problems among these people. Doctors expect long-term health problems, particularly cancer, to increase. What should be done about the problem?

Roles

company president (an American)

factory manager (from the country in which the factory is located)

poor person who lives near the factory

rich person who lives in the capital

local doctor

representative of the national ministry of health

representative of the national ministry for economic development

Quotations

Directions: Read the numbered quotations below and select three from each group with which you most agree. Then follow your teacher's directions.

Quotations about Americans

1. Privacy is important to Americans.
2. Americans believe that time is money.
3. Every American believes that he is equal to everyone else.
4. Americans don't care about the members of their families.
5. Americans don't know their neighbors.
6. American children have too much freedom.
7. Americans are rich.
8. Americans don't know how to relax.
9. Americans are very concerned about weather forecasts.
10. Americans are very independent.

Map Views

Directions: Look at the maps on this page and on p. 46. Then match each map with its "creator" from the list of ministries below. Write the name of the appropriate ministry on the line provided.

Ministries

Defense Economic Development Natural Resources Tourism

Country X

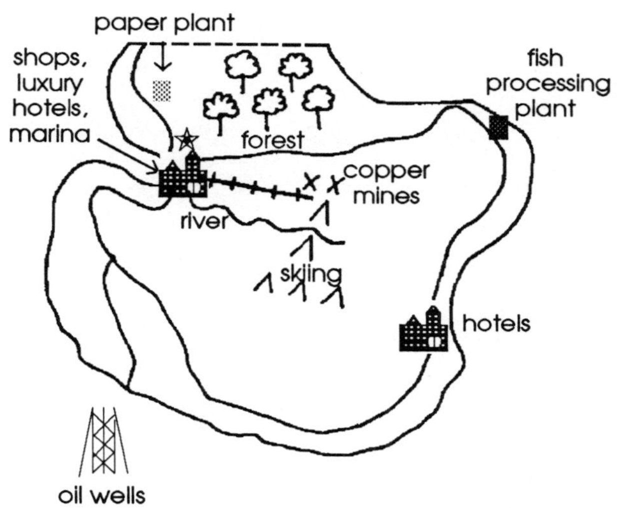

1. ______________________

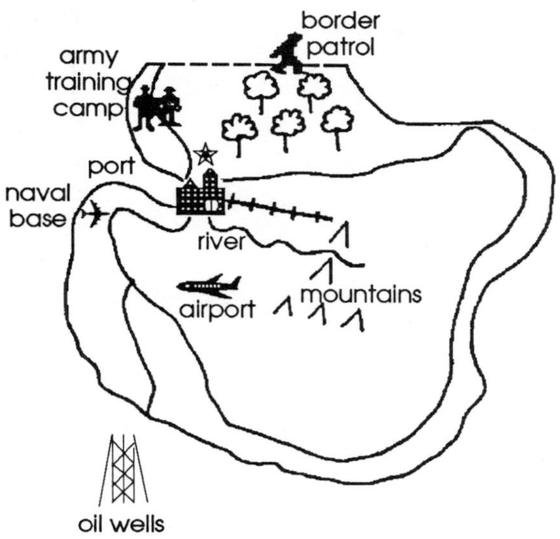

2. ______________________

Continued

Map Views—*Continued*

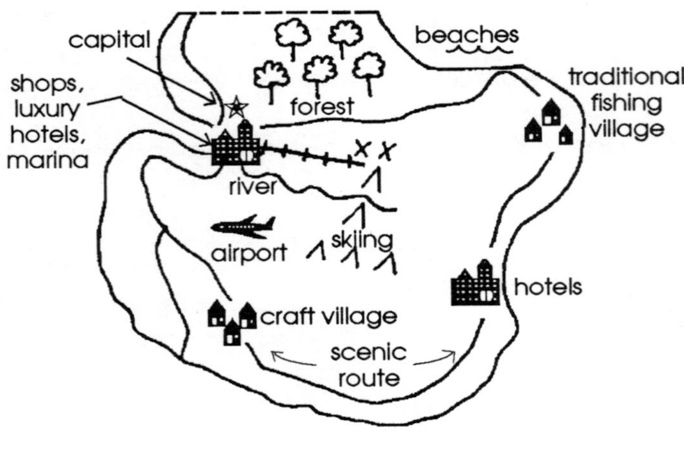

3. ______________________

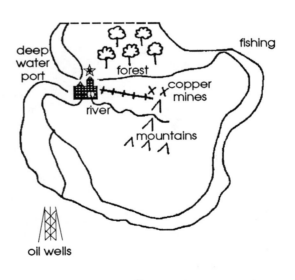

deep water port
forest
fishing
copper mines
river
mountains
oil wells

4. ______________________

Unit 4 Focus

Notes to the Teacher

Introduction

Good writing, like good photography, should have a clear focus. That is, it should not try to show everything about a given subject. Instead it should try to show one part clearly. For many of our students, focusing is a problem since they have been taught to generalize about any given topic. A paragraph about using computers for word processing, for example, might begin with a statement about the benefits of computers to mankind. Other students have a different focus problem. They have learned that to indicate the focus of a paragraph explicitly is to insult the reader's intelligence and reading ability. Rather than explicitly stating the focus, they will provide clues throughout the passage. While a highly skilled writer can work in this fashion, it is unlikely that a novice, especially one writing in a second language, can do so. Such a novice is more likely to end up writing with no focus at all.

A major goal in teaching writing is to help students learn to focus. Indeed, focus is often used as a criterion for judging the level of student writing. As students reach higher levels, we expect them to focus more.

Unit 4

The activities in this unit are intended to give students a sense of what focus means and how to achieve it. Some of the activities require identifying the focus, while others require selecting one.

The Blind Men and the Elephant

Time: 30 minutes
Organization: whole class
Level: intermediate
Materials: *exercise sheet, p. 53*

Distribute copies of the exercise sheet, one per student. Review the directions and answer any questions. When students have finished reading, ask them for comments. Discuss the question at the end of the story. Then ask students to think about the concept of focus. What does the story show about focus? Does the story only apply to blind men and elephants? Ask students for examples of other situations in which a person focuses on one aspect while failing to see the whole.

As a variation, tape the story and present it as a listening activity.

Part of a Whole

Time: 10–15 minutes
Organization: whole class
Level: variable
Materials: a transparency of a picture (see suggestions below); an overhead projector.

Using the overhead projector, cover all but a small part of the transparency. Ask the class to guess what the picture might be. Gradually reveal portions of the picture while pausing to elicit guesses from the class. When the whole picture is visible, ask students to compare it with their original guesses.

An excellent source of pictures that show only a very small part of a whole object ("eyeball benders") is *Games* magazine. The pictures can be numbered and passed among the students individually (or in groups) while they write down their guesses about the subject.

As a variation, show a slide out of focus, and have students guess its content as the slide is gradually brought into focus.

Job Charts

Time: 15–20 minutes the first day, 20–30 minutes the second
Organization: individuals, pairs, whole class
Level: low intermediate
Materials: *exercise sheet, p. 54*

Distribute copies of the exercise sheet, one per student. Review the directions and answer any questions. When students have completed the exercise sheet, have them work in pairs to compare answers. For the next class, ask each student to investigate two or three careers using the exercise sheet as a guide. Information can be obtained from the school career counselor, a teacher, the library, and/or from interviews of people on the job. Students should add the information to their job charts. The following day, draw a large copy of the exercise sheet on the board or on large pieces of paper to be taped on the wall. Have students fill in the information on the careers they investigated. If several students have chosen the same career, they may integrate their information. As a wrap-up, have the whole class discuss the pros and cons of the various jobs.

In more advanced classes students can make their own charts based on a discussion of factors they consider most important in choosing a university (cost, location, majors, size) or buying a car (cost, size, economy, special features).

As a follow-up, have students write a paragraph about the jobs that most interest them.

What Happened?

Time: 20–30 minutes
Organization: small groups (3–4 students)
Level: low intermediate
Material: *exercise sheets, pp. 55–56*; envelopes for storing police reports and clue strips

Distribute the police report strips to each group (see exercise sheets). Explain that the strips together represent two police reports of a woman's death. Police Report A describes the place of the accident and Police Report B describes the events themselves. Students must first separate the sentences for Reports A and B and arrange them in order. Then they must determine what happened. After a few minutes of group discussion, distribute the clue strips, one set per group. Tell students to arrange the clues in order of importance and to use them to help solve the crime.

Step by Step

Time: 20–30 minutes
Organization: whole class, then small groups (3–4 students)
Level: low intermediate
Materials: large sheets of paper; marking pens; tape

Select a process, such as going abroad to study, and brainstorm a list of steps involved (getting information, applying to schools, getting a passport). List the steps on the board and divide the class into groups. Tell the groups to select one step in the process and to write down everything they can think of about it. Next, hand out the paper and marking pens and ask students to sort through their notes and write five or six good sentences about the same step, without identifying the step itself. Tape the sheets of paper around the room and have students walk around reading the sheets and matching them to the steps in the process. As students consider each sheet, have them indicate any sentences they feel are not relevant to the process. Discuss the students' findings.

As a variation, select a more complex topic, such as drugs, and have students, in groups, research one aspect of that topic using the library and/or other available resources.

Matching Paragraphs

Time: 15–25 minutes
Organization: individuals, then pairs and small groups (4 students)
Level: intermediate
Materials: *exercise sheet, p. 57*

Distribute copies of the exercise sheet, one per student. Review the directions and answer any questions. Explain to students that there is one "example" that does not match any of the paragraphs.

When students have completed the exercise sheet, divide the class into pairs to compare answers. Have the pairs discuss personal experiences that could illustrate each paragraph. Merge pairs into groups of four and have each group select one member's experience to illustrate a particular paragraph. Have students share these individual experiences with the class.

Famous Paintings

Time: 20–25 minutes
Organization: whole class, then groups (4–5 students)
Level: high intermediate
Materials: a slide or poster of a famous painting featuring several people; a slide projector and screen (if needed); *exercise sheet, p. 58*

Show the class the slide or poster. Discuss briefly what the painting is about. Then divide the class into groups and distribute copies of the exercise sheet, one per student. Review the directions and answer any questions. Assign each group one of the people shown in the painting. (If the class is large, assign more than one group the same person.)

When the groups have finished writing down the information for their assigned person, have students walk around the room seeking information from each other to complete the exercise sheet for the other people shown in the painting.

I'm the Expert

Time: two classes, 15–25 minutes each
Organization: whole class, then pairs
Level: intermediate
Materials: none

Ask students to think of a topic on which each student is an expert—a hobby, an after-school activity, a sport, and so on. Divide the class into pairs and have students interview each other on their individual area of expertise. Students should take notes on their partner's comments.

Have students write a short composition about their partner for the next class meeting, focusing on the other person's area of expertise. Students should omit from the paper both their own name and the name of the person about whom they are writing.

At the second class meeting, collect the students' papers and number them. Have each student number a blank page according to the number of students in the class. Next, have students read each other's papers and beside each number put the name of the person they think the paper describes. Then, have each student claim the paper written about him or her. Ask students to write on the bottom of the paper any comments to the interviewer regarding the paper's accuracy. Finally, have students return the papers to their interviewers and ask them to check their numbered guesses with the other student interviewers.

Composition Topics

1. When a person goes to live in another country, he or she loses certain things and gains other things. Make a list of what you feel you lost by going to live in another country and another list of what you gained. Then choose one item from each list and write a paragraph about it.

2. Write a paragraph about yourself focusing on some aspect of your personality. For example, you might say, "I have always enjoyed spending time alone." Then give information to support that statement.

3. Educational systems in different countries focus on different kinds of learning. Education in the United States is often described as practical and "hands on," while in many other countries a more theoretical kind of education is offered. Write a composition describing your education up to now.

4. What are the characteristics of a real friend? Write down as many as you can think of. Then choose the one you think is most important and write a paragraph about it.

5. Imagine that you are looking into your room through a window or a hole in the wall. Describe what you see.

6. Look around your room and choose the smallest thing you can see (perhaps a crack in the wall or a fly). Make a list of all the things you could write about it. Then from that list choose one topic and write a paragraph about it.

7. Choose a common object and write a paragraph focusing on one aspect of the object, such as its color(s) or the material(s) of which it is made.

8. Houses all over the world differ in style and materials. List the differences you have noticed between the houses in your native city or town and those where you live now. Then choose one difference (roof design or building material, for example) and write about it.

The Blind Men and the Elephant

Directions: Read the story below and think about the question at the end.

Once upon a time there were four blind men. One day they heard that there was an elephant in town. They all knew the word "elephant," but they did not know what an elephant was like. They decided to go and find out for themselves. The first blind man walked right into the elephant's side. "An elephant is like a wall," he said. "No," said his friend, who had found the elephant's tail. "An elephant is like a rope." "You're both wrong," said the third man, holding the elephant's ear. "An elephant is like a fan." The fourth man had found the elephant's leg. "An elephant is like a tree," he said.

Which one of the men was right?

Job Charts

Directions: Read the job descriptions below. Then fill in the chart with information from the descriptions.

Descriptions

1. I teach English in a high school. My annual pay is $20,000 for the nine-month school year. I go to school at 7:30 every morning and I leave at 4:00 P.M. Every evening I take work home with me. There is a lot of stress in my job because some of the students don't like school. I worry a lot about my students. During the summers I relax with my family.

2. I work in an office as a secretary. My job is not difficult. I do not have a lot of responsibility or stress. I work from 9:00 A.M. to 5:00 P.M. five days a week. I get two weeks of vacation every year. I never take work home with me. My annual pay is $15,000.

3. I am a professional baseball player. My salary is $600,000 a year right now. I don't know what it will be in the future when I am older and can't play as well. There is a lot of stress in my job during spring training and during the baseball season. I have to show every day that I am the best person for my position. I have time off in the winter, but I have to exercise then so that I don't get out of shape.

Job	Pay	Hours	Pros	Cons
1.				
2.				
3.				

What Happened?

Directions to the teacher: Duplicate this exercise sheet and p. 56 and cut along the dotted lines so that each student group receives one complete set of reports (A & B) and clues (•). Then follow the activity directions in the *Notes to the Teacher, p. 49.*

Police Report A:

I turned left into the driveway of the big old house.

The house was dark except for a light in the entrance hall.

The other police cars hadn't arrived yet.

There was a car parked in front of the house.

Out of curiosity I touched the hood.

It was still warm.

I rang the doorbell and the daughter of the victim let me in.

I walked in the front door.

Straight ahead of the door was a big stairway to the second floor.

Immediately in front of me at the base of the stairs lay the body of a woman dressed in a nightgown.

I walked around the body and went upstairs.

At the top of the stairs I found a broken piece of string on the carpet.

Bending down to look closely, I saw a thumbtack stuck in the wood on each side of the stairway.

There was a piece of string attached to each thumbtack.

"She was murdered," I said to myself.

Police Report B:

The victim's daughter called the police at 2 A.M.

We arrived at 2:15 A.M.

We found the victim lying at the bottom of the stairway.

We told the daughter that we wanted to ask her some questions.

First we asked where she was when her mother fell down the stairs.

Continued

What Happened? *Continued*

She told us, "I was in my room sleeping when I heard my mother scream."

Then we asked her to tell us her ideas about what happened.

She said, "Sometimes my mother drank too much. Maybe she was drunk and fell down the stairs."

"What a tragic accident!"

Clue Strips:

The victim had bruises on her upper arms.

The daughter's arms were scratched.

There was skin under the victim's fingernails.

The daughter said she and her mother were home alone all evening.

The victim had deep cuts across her ankles.

The daughter was crying.

The victim was very rich.

Matching Paragraphs

Directions: Read the four paragraphs below and try to identify the main idea of each. Then select a suitable example from those listed, **a** through **e**.

Stress and Living Abroad

When a person goes to live in a foreign country, he finds that the new language causes him a great deal of stress. Even if he has studied the language in his own country, he may find the vocabulary and pronunciation different from what he learned. Furthermore, because the sounds and structures of the new language are unfamiliar to him, he must listen more carefully than he does to his own language.

Although a stranger in a new country feels very lonely, he may find social contacts with the natives of the country a great strain. He is not sure how to behave. This is especially embarrassing to an adult, who already knows how to handle most social situations in his own culture.

Not only are language and social relationships difficult, but a foreigner also has to become accustomed to a new environment in which everyday objects and experiences may be different. The confusion caused by these differences can make even a simple activity seem difficult.

The newcomer also suffers from emotional stress. He has left his family and friends in his own country. He is more alone in the new country than he has ever been in his life. In the process of moving to another country he has left behind much of his own identity. He does not have a family or a job to show who he is. He cannot use the language well enough to show what kind of person he is.

Examples

a. "I am a very shy person," said one recent immigrant.

b. For example, a foreigner finds conversation with a new American friend very tiring. After only ten or fifteen minutes, he finds himself suffering from a terrible headache and a great urge to run away.

c. One foreign student said, "The person you are talking to isn't really me. I don't know English well enough to show you who I am."

d. One illustration is the problem of using a bus. A newcomer to the United States wanted to take a bus downtown. He started to get on the bus by the back door, but the other passengers all yelled at him. In his country, one gets on at the back and pays the person who collects the money. Then he gave the driver a dollar, but she refused to take his money. She told him he needed the exact change. He got off the bus in confusion.

e. For instance, he is not sure what to do when he is introduced to somebody. Is it polite to shake hands? Should he bow? What should he say?

Famous Paintings

Directions: Your teacher will show you a famous painting with several people in it. On the "Name" line below, write the name of each person shown. Then, with your group, fill in the missing information for the person assigned to your group.

Name ______________________

Age ________

Favorite foods ______________________

Hobbies ______________________

Occupation ______________________

Likes ______________________

Dislikes ______________________

Happiest experience ______________________

Worst experience ______________________

Ambition______________________

Name ______________________

Age ________

Favorite foods ______________________

Hobbies ______________________

Occupation ______________________

Likes ______________________

Dislikes ______________________

Happiest experience ______________________

Worst experience ______________________

Ambition______________________

Name ______________________

Age ________

Favorite foods ______________________

Hobbies ______________________

Occupation ______________________

Likes ______________________

Dislikes ______________________

Happiest experience ______________________

Worst experience ______________________

Ambition______________________

Name ______________________

Age ________

Favorite foods ______________________

Hobbies ______________________

Occupation ______________________

Likes ______________________

Dislikes ______________________

Happiest experience ______________________

Worst experience ______________________

Ambition______________________

Organizing Activities

Unit 5 Classification

Notes to the Teacher

Introduction

Classification is the process by which items are grouped together according to some shared characteristic. Every writer needs to develop a sense of which ideas belong together and which do not. Without this sense a writer can produce only a series of disconnected thoughts. Classification, difficult for all novice writers, is further complicated for the foreign student by cultural differences in the criteria used for grouping.

While criteria and categories for grouping may vary from person to person and from culture to culture, they are, nevertheless, answerable to external logic. A student who argues that a bridge belongs with a list of items powered by electricity because it might have lights will find little support among his classmates; but a student who groups stamps and coins with works of art will gain support even if most classmates have not previously considered that possibility.

Sometimes a writer begins with separate ideas among which he must find common links. At other times ideas may be suggested by the categories for grouping. In either case the writer must be able to group items according to externally justifiable criteria.

Unit 5

The purpose of this unit is to give students experience in making classification decisions. The activities in this unit are arranged according to their linguistic complexity. Earlier activities involve students in classifying pictures, objects, and single words, while later activities focus on arranging sentences and paragraphs.

All in Common

Time:	10–20 minutes
Organization:	whole class
Level:	variable
Materials:	none

Ask students to identify characteristics that all members of the class share (for example, course of study, hair and eye color, teachers). List the characteristics on the board. Students may challenge any characteristic listed.

As a variation, have students, working in pairs, small groups, or with the whole class, identify common characteristics in preselected pictures, number series, machines, apparatus or household objects.

Another variation involving the whole class (or groups) is to have one student state a characteristic. Then have the rest of the class identify the people or objects possessing that characteristic.

We're Related

Time:	20–30 minutes
Organization:	large groups (6–10 students), then pairs
Level:	variable
Materials:	a minimum of six magazine pictures for each student, mixed in a pile

Group students in circles around two or three piles of magazine pictures. Ask individual students to pick out three pictures they feel are related. Next ask students, in pairs, to explain their choices to each other. Then have students change partners and repeat the activity several times, each time explaining their choices.

As variations, use photographs, objects, or lists of names of people or items.

Rain, Rain, Go Away

Time:	30 minutes
Organization:	pairs
Level:	high intermediate
Materials:	*exercise sheet, p. 67*

Distribute copies of the exercise sheet, one per student. Review the directions and answer any questions. When each pair has agreed on the three different groups, have them compare their answers with those of another pair.

Connecting Pictures

Time:	20–30 minutes
Organization:	small groups (3–4 students)
Level:	intermediate
Materials:	*exercise sheets, pp. 68–69*; envelope for storing picture cards

This activity is similar to a game of dominoes. Distribute the double picture cards so that each student receives three cards (see exercise sheets). Place one card face up in the middle of each group. Students take turns connecting one of their picture cards to either end of the card displayed. Each student must explain the connection between the two cards. If other students in the group are not satisfied with the explanation for the connection, the student forfeits his or her turn. The first person to connect all three picture cards wins.

As a variation (and a shorter version of the game), use single picture cards instead of double picture cards.

Where's the Milk?

Time:	15–20 minutes
Organization:	small groups (3–4 students)
Level:	low intermediate
Materials:	signs indicating the departments of a supermarket (frozen foods, produce, dairy products, canned fruits and vegetables, meat, fish); newspaper supermarket advertisements; tape

Prior to class, cut out newspaper advertisements for specific items (apples, milk, frozen dinners, and so on). Try to select advertisements featuring pictures, but cut the pictures from the names and prices of the items. Prepare signs for the various supermarket departments and tape them around the room.

In class, give each group six to eight advertisements (with their corresponding pictures). Have students match the pictures and items. Then have each group decide in which department each item belongs. Some items may appear to belong in more than one department. For example, ice cream is both a frozen food and a dairy product. In such cases students must agree on the most logical location. Finally, have each group tape its items under the appropriate supermarket sign. Groups may challenge one another's placements.

As a variation, use the departments and signs of a department store, a hardware, discount or appliance store. Or substitute the kinds of stores themselves and have students indicate what items can be bought at each one.

Lists

Time:	20 minutes per list
Organization:	individual, then pairs and groups (4, 8 students)
Level:	variable
Materials:	*exercise sheet, p. 70*

This activity could easily be done in more than one class period. Since 1. and 2. on the exercise sheet are easier than 3. and 4., the latter two lists could be saved for another class.

Distribute copies of the exercise sheet, one per student. Review the directions and answer any questions. When students have finished comparing their lists, have them work in groups of four, then eight. After a group of four agrees on a classification, students can be asked to reclassify the list using different criteria.

As a variation, use pictures instead of word lists.

Grids

Time:	20–30 minutes
Organization:	pairs
Level:	intermediate
Materials:	*exercise sheets, pp. 71–72*; four separately marked envelopes for storing the word cards

Distribute copies of the grids (p. 71) and the sets of nine word cards each (p. 72). Direct students to place the word cards on their grids so that the words link both horizontally and vertically. Draw the following example on the board and discuss the horizontal and vertical relationships of the words.

zoo	tiger	fur
cage	bird	feathers
tank	fish	fins

When two groups have completed different grids, have them exchange word cards. Continue the activity, as time and interest allow, until all groups have completed four grids.

Puzzle Information

Time: 30 minutes
Organization: pairs
Level: intermediate
Materials: *exercise sheet, p. 73*

Distribute copies of the exercise sheet, one per pair. Review the directions and answer any questions. As students work on the puzzle, intervene as little as possible. Usually somebody can figure out how to solve the problem. If a pair seems to be stuck, suggest the following steps for them to follow:

1. Read all of the information and decide what is useful and what is not.
2. Organize the information on the grid.
3. Test hypotheses and eliminate impossible solutions.
4. Check all answers against the grid.

Outlines

Time: 10–30 minutes, depending on the complexity of the outline
Organization: pairs
Level: high intermediate
Materials: *exercise sheet, p. 74*; envelope for storing outline strips

Distribute the sets of outline strips, one per pair (see exercise sheet). Direct students to organize their strips into an outline, placing subordinate points under main points. By moving strips around, students can try out and discuss different arrangements. Have pairs compare their outlines and/or write a completed outline on the board.

As a variation, take single words that fall naturally into subordinate categories, such as place names (continents, countries, cities), or animal and plant classification schemes, (vertebrates, invertebrates) and organize them into categories and subcategories. More advanced students can work with sentence outlines.

Excuses, Excuses

Time:	20–30 minutes
Organization:	small groups (3–4 students)
Level:	high intermediate
Materials:	*exercise sheet, p. 75*

Try to make sure the groups represent a mixture of nationalities and cultures. Distribute copies of the exercise sheet, one per student. Review the directions and answer any questions. If students disagree on the placement of a number, have the group work together to reach a consensus. When the chart is complete, ask each group to think up and write three additional excuses for each category on the chart.

Composition Topics

1. Write about one way you might classify the people in your country. Some possible categories are religion, language or dialect, origin, income level, social status or region.
2. Write about one way you might classify the students in your school (for example, by academic performance, level, interests, nationality, and so on).
3. Write about the types of friends you have or would like to have.
4. Describe how a year is divided in your country.
5. Describe types of families.
6. Describe the different periods in a person's life.
7. Classify the different holidays in your country (national, religious, and so on).
8. Divide a topic you know well, such as a sport or your field of study, into categories and subcategories.

Rain, Rain, Go Away

Directions: Read the sentences below. Then, with your partner, divide the sentences into three different groups: people who like rain, people who don't like rain, and people who don't say.

"Rain falling on a roof makes a beautiful noise."

"I hate everything about rain. I hate wet shoes and wet hair. I hate wet streets and sidewalks."

"Rain makes me feel peaceful."

"Rain makes me feel angry because it keeps me from doing what I want to do."

"I like rain when I am inside my house."

"Walking in the rain with my girlfriend is very romantic. It's as if we were the only people in the world."

"When I was a child, I hated rain. I had to walk a long way to school and on rainy days my books and papers got soaked. Then my teacher would yell at me. I guess I still feel the same way about rain even though nobody yells at me any more."

"Driving in rain is scary. I don't feel that I can control my car very well."

"Rain is a great treat for me because it doesn't rain very often in my country."

"Without rain we couldn't live. We wouldn't have water to drink or food to eat."

Connecting Pictures

Directions to the teacher: Duplicate this exercise sheet and the one on p. 69 for each group. Next, cut along the dotted lines. Then follow the activity directions in the *Notes to the Teacher, p. 63.*

Continued

Connecting Pictures—*Continued*

Lists

Directions: Read the lists below and classify the items in any way you wish. Then, with a partner, compare lists and agree on a joint list.

1. Food:

milk
coffee
ice cream
chocolate
pizza
hamburgers
peanut butter
breakfast cereal
soda
cookies
spaghetti
potato chips
bread
sandwiches

2. Possessions:

car
toaster
rug
radio
knives and forks
bicycle
refrigerator
television
chair
stove
books
telephone

3. Activities:

washing cars
cutting grass
cooking
changing diapers
repairing cars
earning money
buying food
driving a car
washing dishes
taking children to the park
washing clothes
taking care of young children
buying furniture
cleaning the house

4. Classroom behavior:

arriving late
drinking
laughing
eating
talking to classmates
telling the teacher he or she is wrong
calling the teacher by his or her first name
blowing one's nose
putting one's feet on chairs
reading a newspaper or magazine
leaving the room during class
asking the teacher questions
playing a radio
falling asleep

Grids

Directions to the teacher: Duplicate copies of this exercise sheet and cut along the dotted lines so that each pair receives a grid. Then follow the activity directions in the *Notes to the Teacher, p. 64.*

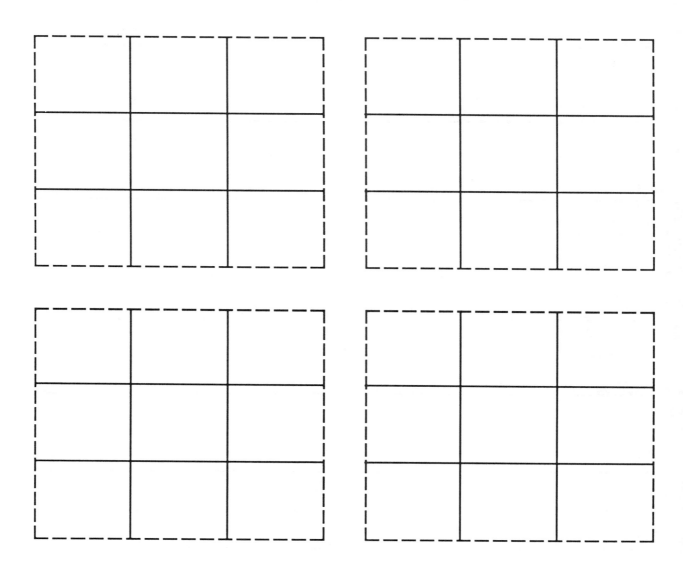

Continued

Grids

Directions to the teacher: Duplicate this exercise sheet and cut along the dotted lines so that each pair receives a different set of nine squares. Then follow the activity directions in the *Notes to the Teacher, p. 64.*

Fire	Stove	Furnace
Wood	Electricity	Gas
Living Room	Kitchen	Basement

Chick	Baby	Puppy
Bird	Human	Dog
Nest	Cradle	Doghouse

Love	Marriage	Home
Joy	Birth	Hospital
Hate	Murder	Prison

Wash	Sleep	Cook
Sink	Bed	Table
Bathroom	Bedroom	Kitchen

Puzzle Information

Directions: Read the story below. Then, with your partner, work out the solutions.

Taiko, Mai-Li, Ana, and Fatima all live in the same apartment building. There are four floors in the building and each woman lives on a different floor. From the information below, decide on which floor each woman lives. Some of the information may not help you.

1. Fatima's husband takes her shopping on Saturdays.
2. Taiko takes off her shoes when she enters her apartment.
3. Taiko lives on a higher floor than Fatima.
4. The husband of the woman who lives on the first floor is a good friend of the husband of the woman who lives on the third floor.
5. The woman on the first floor is very beautiful.
6. Mai-Li lives on the floor between Ana and Fatima.
7. The woman on the first floor works on Saturdays.
8. Only two of the women are married.

Name/Floor	Floor	Married	Saturday Activity
Taiko			
Mai-Li			
Ana			
Fatima			
1st floor			
2nd floor			
3rd floor			
4th floor			

Outlines

Directions to the teacher: Duplicate copies of the sample outline below and cut along the dotted lines so that each student pair receives a complete set of outline strips. Then read the activity directions in the *Notes to the Teacher, p. 65.*

Sample Outline:

Pets are important to people	Production
Companionship	Marketing
To older people	Other pet products
To children	Cages
Protection	Equipment
Watch dogs	Luxuries
Guard snakes	Sweaters
Assistance to the handicapped	Jeweled collars
Guide dogs	Services
Hearing dogs	Haircuts
Monkeys for paraplegics	Medical treatment
Pets are important to business	Veterinarians
Pet food	Psychiatrists

Excuses, Excuses

Directions: Read the list below of excuses for not handing in homework (1–12). Then, with your group, complete the chart, indicating by number which excuses are acceptable, which are not, which are under your control, and which are not.

1. I was too tired.
2. I dropped my homework in the street and a car ran over it.
3. I left it in the library and someone stole it.
4. I forgot to do it.
5. I was feeling homesick.
6. My roommate brought his girlfriend to our room and I had to leave.
7. My sister is in the hospital.
8. The assignment was too hard.
9. I had to pick up my brother at the airport.
10. My neighbor was having a party. It was too noisy to study, so I went to the party.
11. I didn't understand the assignment.
12. I didn't know we had homework.

Excuses	Acceptable	Not acceptable
Student's Fault		
Not Student's Fault		

Unit 6 Sequence

Notes to the Teacher

Introduction

Although there are many ways of organizing our ideas, chronological sequence is probably the most familiar way. When friends ask us how we spent our weekend, we usually give them a chronological account. Similarly, much of what we read in textbooks, especially history and science, is written in chronological order. There are other kinds of sequences as well, such as numerical, geometrical, and spatial.

Unit 6

This unit includes a variety of sequence activities. Some activities ask students to identify and to add to sequences; others require students to create their own sequences.

Next Number

Time: 15–25 minutes
Organization: pairs
Level: low intermediate
Materials: *exercise sheet, p. 83*

Distribute copies of the exercise sheet, one per pair. Review the directions and answer any questions. When students have completed their exercise sheets, have them compare their answers with those of another pair.

Which Came First?

Time: 10 minutes
Organization: pairs
Level: low intermediate
Materials: *exercise sheet, p. 84*

Distribute copies of the exercise sheet, one per pair. Review the directions and answer any questions. When students have completed their exercise sheets, have them compare their answers with those of another student pair.

As a variation, use series of pictures instead of words.

Chinese Horoscope

Time: 20–25 minutes
Organization: pairs or small groups (3 students)
Level: low intermediate
Materials: *exercise sheets, pp. 85-86*

If there are Asian students in the class who know about Chinese horoscopes, include them in different groups. Distribute copies of the exercise sheet, one per pair or group. Review the directions and answer any questions. When students have completed the exercise sheets, have them find their own birth years and read the descriptions. Ask students to discuss the accuracy of the descriptions with their partner or group.

As a follow-up, bring in copies of a local newspaper and have students find and read their own horoscopes. Discuss with the class the different ways people predict the future. Encourage students to comment on whether or not they believe in such predictions.

What Are We Doing?

Time:	10-15 minutes
Organization:	pairs
Level:	intermediate
Materials:	*exercise sheet, p. 87;* envelopes for storing paper strips

Give each pair an envelope containing paper strips (see exercise sheet). Tell students that the paper strips together describe a simple procedure—taking a bath. Each pair should arrange the strips in order, then change partners and compare the results.

As a variation, select a more complex procedure and prepare similar step strips.

As a follow-up, have each student write a paragraph describing the procedure.

What's the Procedure?

Time:	20 minutes
Organization:	small groups (3–4 students)
Level:	intermediate
Materials:	*exercise sheet, p. 88;* tape; envelope for storing sentence strips

Write the following procedure titles on the board: Using Chopsticks, Using a Pay Phone, and Changing a Light Bulb. Distribute one complete set of sentence strips to each group (see exercise sheet). Explain to the groups that they are to determine which of the three procedures identified on the board their sentences describe. Then have students decide the order in which the sentences should appear as steps in the procedure.

After the groups have confirmed that the sentences are in the correct order, students should try to fill in the blanks with appropriate words. Finally, have each group write its procedure on the board, leaving blanks for the words the group couldn't provide. Review each of the completed written procedures with the entire class.

As a variation, use school-related procedures, such as checking books out of the school library, fire drills, using the cafeteria, and so on. Directions to familiar places in the school neighborhood can also be used.

You Tell Me

Time: 30 minutes
Organization: pairs
Level: high intermediate
Materials: none

Ask students to think of something they know how to do; for example, swim, sew on a button, check a book out of a library. Allow a few minutes for students to write down the steps involved in the activity. Assign each student a partner. Have students tell their partners what activity is being described and the steps associated with it. Partners should listen and suggest ways to make the description clearer. When both partners have presented their descriptions and received feedback, have students change partners. This time students should present their activity steps without first identifying the activity itself. Partners must identify the activity on the basis of the steps described.

As a follow-up, have students write down their activity steps in paragraph form. More advanced students can write down their partner's activity steps.

Comic Strips

Time: 10-15 minutes
Organization: pairs or small groups (2–3 students)
Level: intermediate
Materials: different comic strips cut into frames, one complete strip per group (The longer Sunday strips are preferable because they have more frames and are printed in a larger format.); envelope for storing comic strip frames

Distribute the comic strips and/or allow students to choose their favorite one, one strip per group. Tell the groups to arrange the frames in order. Then combine two groups and have each group present its comic strip story to the other. Alternatively, each group can write down its story. More advanced students can tell the story using indirect speech.

As a variation, give each student in a group one comic strip frame. Students must decide on the sequence of the frames based on oral descriptions only. When a sequence has been decided, students can show each other their frames and check on the accuracy of the sequence.

Another variation makes use of other picture sequences, such as those appearing in many self-instruction books. Students can then provide the verbal instructions that might accompany the pictures.

Inventing History

Time: 15–20 minutes
Organization: pairs, then small groups (4 students)
Level: low intermediate
Materials: any object or article of clothing

Bring an object of any kind to class and tell the students that it has a very interesting history. Students must decide what the object's history is. If the object is new, they can trace its path from raw materials to final product. If the object is old, students can talk about its previous owners or about its history. After ten minutes, combine pairs into fours to compare stories.

As a variation, make up a story about the object and have students elicit the story by asking questions. Or, have students in groups write down their own "object" stories. Duplicate and distribute these stories for another class meeting.

Composition Topics

1. Write a paragraph describing the steps involved in using a specific machine, such as an automatic teller, a vending machine, a pay phone, a coin-operated washing machine or a copy machine.
2. Choose an important day in your life. Write down everything that happened to you on that day, in chronological order.
3. Choose an important event in the history of your country. Write a paragraph about the events that led up to it or about those that occurred as a result of it.
4. Choose three adjectives that describe your personality. Write them down in order of importance. Write a paragraph explaining how each one describes you.
5. Describe a day in which everything went wrong. Write about it in chronological order.
6. Using a guidebook, plan a three-day trip to a city you have never visited. Write a short composition about your plans for each day. In planning, consider such factors as weather, opening and closing times, transportation, distances, and so on.
7. Choose a mathematics problem that is difficult for you to solve. As you solve it, write down the steps you follow. Write a paragraph describing those steps.
8. "Man Eaten by Bear in Park"—choose this or another newspaper headline and tell the story behind it. Start with the end result and work backwards through the steps that led up to it.

Next Number

Directions: With your partner, read the number series below and the explanations that follow them. Then match the explanations to the series and write the next number in each series on the blank provided.

NUMBER SERIES

1. 9 | 10 | 8 | 9 | 7 | 8 | 6 | ____
2. 13 | 26 | 78 | 312 | ____
3. 8 | 9 | 11 | 12 | 14 | 15 | 17 | ____
4. 37 | 42 | 34 | 39 | 31 | ____
5. 32 | 40 | 47 | 53 | 58 | ____
6. 14 | 42 | 49 | 147 | 154 | ____
7. 29 | 35 | 47 | 65 | ____
8. 41 | 52 | 64 | 75 | 87 | 98 | ____

EXPLANATIONS

a. Add 1 to the first number, then add 2.

b. Add 8 to the first number, then add 7 to the sum of those two. Continue to add to the total, decreasing by 1 the number added each time.

c. Add 1 to the first number, subtract 2 from the total.

d. Add 6 to the first number. Continue to add multiples of 6 (12, 18, etc.)

e. Multiply the first number by 2, the second number by 3, etc., adding 1 each time to the number by which you are multiplying.

f. Add 5 to the first number, subtract 8 from the next.

g. Add 11 to the first number and 12 to the next.

h. Multiply the first number by 3. Add 7 to the product.

Which Came First?

Directions: With your partner, arrange each numbered series of words in chronological order. Be prepared to explain your sequence.

1. planes, carriages, rockets, cars, horses

____

____

____

____

____

2. refrigerators, microwave ovens, washing machines, dishwashers

____

____

____

____

3. atomic clocks, watches, sundials, wall clocks

____

____

____

4. iron tools, stone tools, bronze tools

____

____

____

5. VCRs, radio, television, tape recorders, phonographs

____

____

____

____

6. clubs, bows and arrows, rifles

____

____

____

Chinese Horoscope

Directions: With your partner or group, read the descriptions below. Decide what the missing year is and write it in the blank.

Ox
1937, 19____, 1961, 1973
You are a leader. You are smart and cheerful. You are compatible with the snake and cock. Your opposite is the sheep.

Tiger
1938, 1950, 19____, 1974
You are honest and sensitive. You are brave. You are compatible with the horse and dog. Your opposite is the monkey.

Boar
19____, 1959, 1971, 1983
Your friends are very faithful to you. You are compatible with the rabbit and sheep. Your opposite is the snake.

Monkey
1944, 1956, 19____, 1980
You try to be the best. You are intelligent. You are compatible with the dragon and the rat. Your opposite is the tiger.

Dragon
19____, 1952, 1964, 1976
You are strong and emotional. Your life is not simple. You are compatible with the monkey. Your opposite is the dog.

Dog
1946, 1958, 19____, 1982
You are generous and loyal. You work well with others. You are compatible with the horse and the tiger. Your opposite is the dragon.

Horse
1942, 1954, 1966, 19____
You are attractive and popular. You are compatible with the tiger and dog. Your opposite is the rat.

Rat
1948, 1960, 19____, 1984
You are ambitious and sincere. You are generous. You are compatible with the dragon and monkey. Your opposite is the horse.

Sheep
1943, 19____, 1967, 1979
You are stylish and love beauty. You are a private person. You are compatible with the boar and the rabbit. Your opposite is the ox.

Cock
1945, 1957, 19____, 1981
You are looking for wisdom and truth. You have a pioneering spirit. You are compatible with the snake and ox. Your opposite is the rabbit.

Snake
1941, 1953, 1965, 19____
You are strong-willed. You show great wisdom. You are compatible with the ox and the cock. Your opposite is the boar.

Rabbit
1939, 1951, 19____, 1975
You are talented and loving. You like peace and quiet. You are compatible with the sheep and the boar. Your opposite is the cock.

Continued

Chinese Horoscope *Continued*

Directions: Review the descriptions on the preceding page (p. 85). Then on this page write the name of the animal shown and its next year in the horoscope on the line below each picture.

What Are We Doing?

Directions to the teacher: Duplicate copies of this exercise sheet for each student pair in the class. Cut along the dotted lines and put the paper strips in an envelope. Then follow the activity directions in the *Notes to the Teacher, p. 79.*

take off clothes	sit down
turn on faucet	apply soap all over body
put in plug	rinse off
wait	stand up
fill the tub	take out plug
turn off faucet	step out
step in	

What's the Procedure?

Directions to the teacher: Duplicate this exercise sheet and cut along the dotted lines so that each student receives one sentence strip. (If there are more than 20 students in your class, repeat one of the sequences or create your own.) Then, follow the activity directions in the *Notes to the Teacher, p. 79*.

Hold one ____________ as you would hold a pencil. Pressing ____________ with your thumb against ____________ middle and index fingers.

While still holding the first ____________, put the ____________ chopstick between your middle ____________ and the base of your ____________.

Keep the ____________ firmly in place with ____________ end of your fourth ____________.

Now hold the chopsticks ____________, tips down, just above your ____________.

Place the tip of ____________ second chopstick under the ____________ and grasp it firmly.

Find a telephone ____________.

Pick up the ____________ and insert the necessary ____________.

____________ the number.

If the line is busy, ____________.

Be sure to check ____________ return slot to get your ____________ back.

Be sure that the ____________ is turned OFF.

Remove the old ____________ carefully.

____________ in the new light bulb.

Turn it carefully ____________ firmly until it is tight.

Turn the light ____________.

Organizing

Unit 7 Cause and Effect

Notes to the Teacher

Introduction

For many students, native as well as non-native English speakers, cause and effect relationships are difficult to understand. Causes become mixed with effects, and, in some cases, chronological relationships are confused with causal ones. While cause and effect relationships may be troublesome, understanding them is essential for students entering academic careers in any field. Not only are students expected to understand explicitly stated cause and effect relationships, but they are also expected to be able to formulate their own cause and effect statements.

Cause and effect relationships can be practiced using almost any information, ranging from everyday occurrences (John came to class late) to sophisticated technical data. They are, therefore, easily worked into class activities at any time. Because an understanding of causal relationships is so essential, it is important to study them.

Unit 7

The activities in this unit ask students to distinguish cause from effect, to formulate causes and/or effects for given information, and to weigh conflicting consequences.

Riddles

Time: 10 minutes
Organization: whole class and small groups (2–3 students)
Level: intermediate
Materials: *exercise sheet, p. 95*

Save copies of the exercise sheet for distribution, one per student, at the end of class. Select a riddle from the exercise sheet and read it aloud once or twice to the whole class. Then divide the class into groups. Have the group members first check their understanding of the riddle, then try to solve it together. When all groups have solved the first riddle, have them share their answers and explanations with the whole class. Continue with other riddles from the exercise sheet as time and interest allow. Then distribute the copies of the exercise sheet.

Match Me

Time: 10–15 minutes
Organization: individual students
Level: intermediate
Materials: *exercise sheets, p. 96*; envelope for storing sentence strips

Distribute the sentence strips, one per student (see exercise sheet). Then tell students to each find another student whose strip could be combined with theirs (using an appropriate connector) to form a cause and effect sentence. When students have found their matching strips, have them write the resulting sentences on the board, inserting the appropriate connector and adjusting punctuation and capitalization as necessary. Then have the class identify the cause and the effect in each sentence and point out any sentences that appear illogical. Many of the strips can be interpreted as either cause or effect depending on how they are used.

Crazy Poem

Time: 15–20 minutes
Organization: pairs
Level low intermediate
Materials: *exercise sheet, p. 97*

Distribute copies of the exercise sheet, one per student. Review the directions and answer any questions. Then have students repeat the poem after you in the manner of a "jazz chant." Divide the class into pairs to complete the exercise sheet. When students have finished explaining the illogical statements to their partners, have them form new pairs to compare answers.

As a follow-up, present the lyrics of the Stephen Foster song "Oh Susannah" or create illogical statements using other classroom material.

Here's Why

Time: 10–15 minutes
Organization: whole class, then pairs
Level: variable
Materials: *exercise sheet, p. 98*

Distribute copies of the exercise sheet, one per student. Review the directions and answer any questions. At the end of class have students compare explanations.

Tell Me Why

Time: 10–30 minutes
Organization: pairs
Level: low intermediate
Materials: *exercise sheet, p. 99*

Distribute copies of the exercise sheet, one per student. Review the directions and answer any questions. After all of the pairs have answered the questions, have them compare their answers with those of other pairs. Then read and discuss the explanations provided in the Answer Key (p. 118).

Finish the Story

Time: variable
Organization: whole class
Level: high intermediate
Materials: a transparency of *exercise sheet, p. 100*; an overhead projector

Before beginning this activity, explain to students that you are going to show them a story, sentence by sentence. As students read each sentence, they are to predict the cause or effect of the statement and to finish it by adding some words. Then project the first part of the exercise sheet/story on the board, covering the rest of the story with a piece of paper. Ask students to suggest as many ways as they can to continue the story. In the space provided on the transparency, write the suggestion the students like best. Then reveal the next part of the story and have students compare the completed statement with their suggestion. Work through the rest of the story, sentence by sentence, stopping wherever causal connectors appear, to allow students to finish the sentence.

As a follow-up, have students copy the first sentence of the story, then rewrite the rest of the story using their own sentences.

The Way We Said It

Time: two days, 15–20 minutes each
Organization: individuals, then small groups (2–3 students)
Level: high intermediate
Materials: large sheets of paper; marking pens; tape

Using large sheets of paper, copy the following quotations, leaving space for students to write in their own sentences:

"It takes me a long time to write a short paragraph."
"I have trouble selecting an appropriate topic."
"The hardest thing for me is spelling."
"Before I write a composition in English, I write it first in my native language."
"Ideas for writing all get mixed together in my head."

Tape the sheets around the room and leave a marking pen near each sheet. Ask students to walk around the room reading the quotations. Then have students write cause and effect statements on

The Way We Said It — *Continued*

the quotation sheets of their choice. (Correct any grammatical errors yourself or have students correct them.) Prior to the next class meeting, make copies of the students' cause and effect statements. At the next class meeting, divide students into groups and distribute the statement sheets, one per group. Ask the groups to identify the quotation to which each statement pertains. Then ask students to specify whether the statement is a cause or an effect of the related quotation.

As a follow-up, have students write about a quotation with which they identify.

Those Puzzling Americans

Time:	two days, 15–20 minutes each
Organization:	whole class, pairs
Level:	high intermediate
Materials:	none

In this activity, students select a puzzling aspect of American life and ask Americans their opinions about it. The activity is most effective if the question relates directly to material or lessons under study and represents something about which students are genuinely puzzled. For example, foreign students often ask "Why do many American young people move away from their parents before they are married?" On the first day, ask students to brainstorm possible questions and to agree on one to ask. Then have them decide how many people to ask and whether to conduct the survey individually or in pairs. On the second day, have students bring in the answers they received to their question and have one student write the answers on the board. Students should identify and correct any errors in their sentences. Next divide the class into pairs. Tell the pairs to look for similar answers and to group them together. Then have students write a paragraph, arranging the sentences in logical order and adding linking words as needed.

As a follow-up, duplicate and distribute copies of the students' paragraphs and have students compare and evaluate them.

Composition Topics

1. Think of a child's question such as: Why is the sky blue? or Why is the grass green? Write an answer to the question.
2. Why did you come to the US? List your reasons in the order of importance. Choose the most important one and write about it or write about all of them in the order of their importance.
3. Why do students fail?
4. What are the major causes of car accidents? You might choose a specific group of drivers (young people, old people, men, women, etc.).
5. "Give a man a fish and he has food for one meal. Teach a man to fish and he has food for a lifetime." This is a cause and effect statement. Explain it.
6. It is said that Americans are culturally isolated; that is, they see only their own culture. What do you think are some causes of this? What are some results?
7. What would happen if we did not have a police force?
8. Why do cars have license plates?

Riddles

Directions: Your teacher will read these riddles (1–6) aloud to you in class. Compare your answers with those your teacher gives you.

Riddles

1. A bear goes for a walk. He walks ten miles south, ten miles east and ten miles north, returning to his starting point. What color is the bear?
2. Mr. Jones tells everyone that he is the brother of a famous scientist. However, Mr. Jones doesn't have a brother. Even so, he is telling the truth. How is this possible?
3. A bus driver went down a street and passed a stop sign without stopping. He turned left where there was a no left turn sign. Then he went the wrong way on a one way street. Yet, he didn't break a single traffic law. Why not?
4. Mr. Miller was lonely and decided to buy a bird for company. He went to a pet store. The owner showed him a beautiful parrot. "This bird will repeat any word it hears," said the owner. Mr. Miller was very excited and he bought the bird. When he got it home, he talked to it, but the bird never said a word. He took the bird back to the pet store. "You lied to me," Mr. Miller told the owner. "No, I didn't," answered the owner. The owner was telling the truth. How is this possible?
5. Two fathers and two sons went fishing. Each of them caught one fish. However, the total number of fish was only three. How is this possible?
6. John walked downtown in one hour and fifteen minutes. Coming back to his house he didn't walk any faster and he didn't take any shortcuts, but it only took him seventy-five minutes. How is this possible?

Match Me

Directions to the teacher: Duplicate this exercise sheet and cut along the dotted lines so that each student receives a sentence strip. Then follow the activity directions in the *Notes to the Teacher, p. 90*.

John lost his job	He got to the airport late
Mary left the party early	My car is wrecked
Michael ran away from home	The neighbors complained
He gave his car to a friend	I smoke three packs of cigarettes a day
She didn't have enough money to pay for dinner	He was late for class
She bought an elephant	He didn't get home until 3 A.M.
He didn't write to his parents last week	He got drunk
She bought new furniture last week	I have a bad cough
She ran out of money	My car is in the garage
She called her parents and talked for an hour	He borrowed $1,000 from a friend

Crazy Poem

Directions: Read the poem below aloud, following your teacher's example. Then work with your partner to identify any illogical or "crazy" statements.

I got up early this morning, about twelve o'clock.
I looked out the window and I had a shock.
The sun was shining brightly, it was raining
everywhere,
The trees were walking up and down, their roots
were in the air.
I got dressed and took a shower,
Froze some coffee and ate a flower.
Then I hurried to the street,
where a boat passed by my feet.

Here's Why

Directions: Read each statement below. Then find another student and read one of the statements to him or her. Listen to the explanation your classmate gives and write it in the space provided.

1. You didn't invite us to your party. ______________________
2. You didn't do your homework. ______________________
3. You didn't call your parents. ______________________
4. You didn't pay your rent. ______________________
5. You didn't pick me up last night. ______________________
6. You didn't bring your book to class. ______________________
7. You didn't send your friend a birthday card. ______________________
8. You didn't bring paper to class. ______________________
9. You don't have car insurance. ______________________
10. You refused to lend me your car. ______________________
11. You didn't clean up your room. ______________________
12. You don't have a valid driver's license. ______________________

Tell Me Why

Directions: With your partner, try to answer each of the questions (1-6) below. Write your answers on the line below each question. Ask your teacher if you need help with any of the vocabulary.

1. Why does my voice sound different when it is recorded?

   ____

2. Why will a cooked egg stand on end and a raw one will not?

   ____

3. Why are mountain tops cold? Don't they get the same amount of heat from the sun as the ground does?

   ____

4. Why are the bottoms of some pie pans painted black?

   ____

5. Why do people in tropical climates wear light-colored clothes?

   ____

6. Why is there less damage to plants on a cold day if they are covered with snow?

   ____

Finish the Story

Directions to the teacher: Before beginning this activity, make a transparency of this exercise sheet. Then follow the activity directions in the *Notes to the Teacher, p. 92.*

I was driving in the desert late one afternoon, trying to reach my home town before it got dark. I was in a hurry to get there so I could . . .

attend my sister's wedding. Before I left the city, I had forgotten to fill my car with gas. I felt very stupid when . . .

my car ran out of gas. I got out of the car in order to . . .

walk to the next town. I saw a truck coming toward me and I . . .

waved at it, but it didn't stop because . . .

it was going too fast. I continued walking down the road until it started getting so dark that . . .

I was afraid I might get lost. Therefore I . . .

lay down next to the road to sleep. I woke up because . . .

I felt a large snake slithering across me. That made me jump up and . . .

run away. I ran so fast that I . . .

fell down and hit my head very hard on a large rock. I woke up to the sound of music. Everybody around me was singing because . . .

it was my sister's wedding.

Unit 8 Comparison and Contrast

Notes to the Teacher

Introduction

In academic as well as in everyday life, we make comparisons and contrasts. In doing so, we have to establish specific criteria against which to measure or judge something. For example, if we are buying a house, we might consider price and/or size as well as location and/or condition. Beyond establishing criteria, we must limit and prioritize them.

In comparison and contrast essays, many foreign students find it difficult to establish criteria and to limit and prioritize them. Their essays often consist of separate, general descriptions of objects without showing their relation to each other. Either the criteria for comparison and contrast have not been clearly identified or a systematic point by point comparison/contrast has not been made.

Unit 8

The activities in this unit offer students practice in identifying criteria and in using them to make comparisons and contrasts.

Similarities and Differences

Time: 10–15 minutes
Organization: whole class
Level: low intermediate
Materials: a picture or an object for each member of the class, such as a key, a ring, a flashbulb, a pencil, a pair of glasses, a measuring cup, a piece of candy, a roll of tape, a plastic cup, a small box, a watch, a comb, a pair of scissors, a cassette, a can opener, a bottle cap

Pass out the items or pictures or let students provide their own. Then direct students to compare their object with that of another student, noting the similarities and differences. At a given signal from you (for example, flashing the classroom lights), have students find another student with whom to again compare objects. Continue the activity until all students have talked to one another or, if your class is large, until you feel it is time to stop. Then ask students to stand next to the person whose object most resembles their own. Finally, ask students to stand next to the person whose object least resembles theirs. Ask the class to suggest possible similarities between the various pairs of objects.

Opinions

Time: variable
Organization: pairs
Level: high intermediate
Materials: sets of two reviews of the same movie, book or car, or letters to the editor concerning a particular issue from a magazine or newspaper. The reviews or letters should reflect opposing views, at least in part.

Distribute the sets of reviews or letters to each pair, giving each student a different review or letter to read. (Different pairs may work with different sets of reviews or letters.) Ask students to take turns summarizing the main points of the review or letter for their partner. Then ask each pair to write down the main points of similarity and difference between the two reviews or letters.

As a variation, try tape-recording or videotaping opinions expressed on different issues, topics, or films. Or, consult *Consumer Reports*, *Car and Driver*, and *Motor Trend* for reports on different products, cars, and so on.

Country X and the U.S.

Time:	15–20 minutes
Organization:	small groups (3–4 students)
Level:	low intermediate
Materials:	*exercise sheet, p. 107*

Distribute copies of the exercise sheet, one per student. Review the directions and answer any questions. Explain to students that upon completing the exercise they will have two statements about the United States left over. Students should write contrasting statements to go with them.

Descriptions

Time:	30–40 minutes
Organization:	whole class, with five students sent out of the room
Level:	intermediate
Materials:	a large picture or poster

Send five students out of the classroom. While they are gone, show the class the item, a picture or poster. Then conceal the item and call back one student. Ask the rest of the class to describe the item to the student. Ask the student to describe the item to the second student called back. Repeat the procedure until all five students have returned to the classroom and have received *and given* a description of the item. Show the picture or poster to the entire class and have students compare the fifth student's description to the picture itself.

As a variation, use a story or ask the last student to draw the picture or poster on the board as described.

Matching Proverbs

Time: 20-30 minutes
Organization: pairs, then small groups (4 students)
Level: high intermediate
Materials: *exercise sheet, pp. 108–109*

Distribute copies of the exercise sheet, one per pair. Review the directions and answer any questions. When pairs have completed the exercise sheet, have them compare answers with those of another pair.

As a follow-up, have students select their favorite proverb regarding friendship, explaining the reason for their selection.

Finish My Sentence

Time: 30 minutes
Organization: whole class
Level: high intermediate
Materials: none

On the board write the beginning of a sentence, such as "You know you are successful when . . ." or "World peace is possible only if . . ." Ask students to think of an ending for the sentence and have them write their endings on the board. Next ask the class to identify and to eliminate sentences that express the same idea. Then ask students to identify sentences that are similar. Finally ask students to compare the different viewpoints presented.

Men and Women

Time: 30-40 minutes
Organization: small groups (3–5 students)
Level: high intermediate
Materials: *exercise sheet, p. 110*

Distribute copies of the exercise sheet, one per student. Be sure that each member of the same group receives the same half of the exercise sheet. Do not tell students there are two versions of the story. Review the directions and answer any questions. After all groups have reached a decision, have them share their solutions. Compare the solutions made for Jim with those made for Jane. Consider how the sex of the main character may have influenced the groups' decisions.

It's Our Custom

Time: 20–30 minutes
Organization: individuals, then groups, then pairs
Level: intermediate
Materials: none

Select one aspect of culture to compare, such as eating, introductions, or the use of names. Direct students to write down their culture's rules about this aspect and to compare notes with other students in the class from the same culture. Then pair students with classmates from other cultures and have them discuss and list the similarities and differences in their customs. If all students are from the same country, have them write down their understanding of the rules. Next ask them to guess how people in a different culture behave (for example, Americans, British, French). Then, if possible, show a film of the behavior of people in that culture. Ask students in pairs to compare and contrast observed behaviors with their own behavior.

A Dilemma

Time: 30 minutes
Organization: groups (4–5 students), then whole class
Level: high intermediate
Materials: *exercise sheet, p. 111*

Distribute copies of the exercise sheet, one per student. Review the directions and answer any questions. When all groups have completed the exercise sheet, have each group present its solution to the class.

As a follow-up, assign a composition in which students explain which country they would prefer to work in and why.

Who Should Get the Money?

Time: 1 hour
Organization: small groups (3–4 students)
Level: high intermediate
Materials: *exercise sheet, p. 112*

Distribute copies of the exercise sheet, one per student. Review the directions and answer any questions. After giving the groups 20 minutes to discuss the problem, announce that, due to insufficient funding, the total amount available will be cut to $750,000. Allow another 20 minutes for groups to revise their decisions. Then create a chart on the board and have each group indicate its preference for projects. Use the chart as a focus for discussing the various projects and choices.

Composition Topics

1. Choose two words with similar meanings. Then write a paragraph telling how the words are similar and how they are different. Here are some ideas: table/chair, knife/scissors, cat/dog, car/bus, friend/acquaintance, king/president.
2. In the United States television is paid for by advertising. In many countries it is paid for by the government. Make a list of the advantages and disadvantages of each system. Then choose the most important advantage and disadvantage of each system. Write two paragraphs explaining each one of your choices.
3. Choose a current event. Tell how your country's view of it differs from that of the United States.
4. "Why don't Americans speak English the way my English teacher at home did?" Describe the differences between the way your teacher talked and the way most Americans talk.
5. Compare the classroom behavior of Americans to that of students in your country.
6. Ask five people their views on capital punishment and compare them with your own.
7. "The policeman is your friend." Do you agree with this statement? Compare your opinion with those of two or three other people.
8. Compare the breakfasts below in terms of nutritional value, convenience, and taste:

a. tea	b. tea	c. coffee	d. coffee with milk
soup	cheese	bacon	bread
pickles	olives	eggs	
	bread	toast	

Country X and the U.S.

Directions: Read each statement below. With your group decide which statements refer to the United States and which refer to Country X. Then contrast the two countries on given topics, such as food, weather, and so on.

1. We eat a lot of fresh fruit and vegetables but not a lot of meat.
2. It's so easy to drive. I got my license the first time I took the test.
3. We eat rice every day.
4. I couldn't believe it when I saw girls in my classes wearing short pants.
5. It costs 75¢ to ride on a bus. That doesn't even count buying a transfer.
6. Men don't usually do household chores.
7. The weather is always warm.
8. The food in the dormitory is really a problem. They serve a lot of potatoes, but they hardly ever have rice.
9. My brother and I have learned to cook and wash our own clothes since we came here.
10. Public transportation is very cheap.
11. I was surprised when I went shopping for food. Meat is very inexpensive, but the cost of fresh fruits and vegetables is high.
12. When I came here, it was winter. I thought I was in a dead city.

Matching Proverbs

Directions: Read the proverbs (1–25) below. Then, with your partner, match those proverbs that are similar in meaning and those that are opposite in meaning and write the numbers of each on the lines below.

Proverb	Similar	Different
1. Absence makes the heart grow fonder.	________	________
2. Lend your money and lose a friend.	________	________
3. Before you make a friend, eat with him.	________	________
4. Friends tie their purse with a cobweb thread.	________	________
5. Life without friends is death.	________	________
6. Out of sight, out of mind.	________	________
7. A friend in need is a friend indeed.	________	________
8. The best mirror is an old friend.	________	________
9. Misfortune makes enemies of friends.	________	________
10. One enemy is too many, one hundred friends are too few.	________	________
11. A friend to everybody is a friend to nobody.	________	________
12. A rich man doesn't know who his friend is.	________	________
13. Try your friend before you trust.	________	________

Continued

Matching Proverbs — *Continued*

Proverb	Similar	Different
14. A friend is equal to a brother.		
15. Friends are thieves of time.		
16. Friends agree best at a distance.		
17. When a friend asks, there is no tomorrow.		
18. I cannot be your friend and your flatterer too.		
19. A friend is another self.		
20. Poor folks' friends soon forget them.		
21. You are known by the company you keep.		
22. Treat your friend as if he might become your enemy.		
23. Show me his friends and I will tell you who he is.		
24. Wealth maketh many friends.		
25. Birds of a feather flock together.		

Men and Women

Directions to the teacher: Duplicate, cut, and distribute this exercise sheet so that half of the groups receive the story about Jim and half the story about Jane. Then follow the activity directions in the *Notes to the Teacher, p. 104.*

Jim Moore works as a sales representative for a large corporation. He has been offered a promotion with a higher salary and more responsibility. He will be regional sales representative, supervising other sales people. The new job will require longer working hours. In addition, he will have to go out of town at least two days every week. Jim is very excited about the offer, but he is not sure if he should be away from his wife and two small children so much. His wife also works and the children are taken care of by a babysitter. The babysitter is a very responsible woman whom the children like. Jim does not have to accept the promotion. What do you think he should do?

Jane Moore works as a sales representative for a large corporation. She has been offered a promotion with a higher salary and more responsibility. She will be regional sales representative, supervising other sales people. The new job will require longer working hours. In addition, she will have to go out of town at least two days every week. Jane is very excited about the offer, but she is not sure if she should be away from her husband and two small children so much. Her husband also works and the children are taken care of by a babysitter. The babysitter is a very responsible woman whom the children like. Jane does not have to accept the promotion. What do you think she should do?

A Dilemma

Directions: Read the situation below. Then, with your group, discuss the best solution to the problem.

Job Dilemma

A student from Country X is studying in Country Y. He is trying to decide whether to remain in Country Y or to return to his homeland. He has the following information to help him decide:

Country X:

- Promotions and pay are based on age and years of employment.
- A new employee begins by working in his general field, but not in his specialty.
- Well-trained people in his field are needed.
- His family lives in X.
- Salaries are low in X, but he can earn enough to live comfortably.
- Retirement and health insurance are provided by the government.
- Country X does not have the sophisticated equipment he is trained to use.

Country Y:

- Promotions and pay are based on education and skills.
- He will work as a specialist from the beginning.
- There are many well-trained people in his field.
- He has friends in Y.
- Salaries are higher than in X, but so is the cost of living.
- He will have to pay for retirement and health insurance.
- Country Y has good facilities for his work.

Who Should Get the Money?

Directions: You and your group are part of a special committee. You must decide how to spend $1,000,000. Read about the eight worthy projects below and decide together how to spend the money.

Grants for education in city schools, including producing two films. $300,000	Funds to support a hospice for terminally ill lung patients. $600,000
Funds for a lobbyist to persuade the government to make laws limiting smoking in public places and banning televised cigarette commercials. $85,000	Funds to support special care facilities for premature babies of smokers. $500,000
Disability benefits for sufferers of lung disease caused by smoking. $500,000	Sponsorship of a national TV anti-smoking campaign. $450,000
Grant for research on the effects of second-hand smoke on non-smokers. $100,000	Funds to help establish a respiratory intensive care unit in a regional hospital. $450,000

Answer Key

Answer Key

Unit 1 **Audience**

Audience, Audience (p. 13)

1. d **2.** b **3.** f **4.** e **5.** a **6.** c

Unit 2 **Purpose**

Road Signs (p. 27)

1. food, gas/to inform **2.** no right turn/to order **3.** picnic area/to inform **4.** no U turn/to order **5.** no left turn /to order **6.** merging traffic/to warn **7.** camping/to inform **8.** pedestrian crossing/to warn **9.** railroad crossing /to warn

Purpose Questions (p. 28)

Note: Answers will vary depending on the contexts imagined; answers in parentheses might also be acceptable.

1. a (b, f, g) **2.** c (f, g) **3.** g (d) **4.** f (a, c) **5.** h (a, g) **6.** a (g) **7.** a (c, f) **8.** a (c, f, g) **9.** f (d) **10.** e (g, h) **11.** e(g) **12.** a (f, g)

A Word About Smoking (p. 31)

1. c **2.** a **3.** a **4.** b **5.** c **6.** b **7.** a **8.** b **9.** c **10.** a **11.** b

Unit 3 **Point of View**

Family Tree (p. 39)

1. Michael or Jim **2.** Mary **3.** Peter **4.** Jane **5.** Lisa **6.** Peter **7.** Art **8.** John **9.** Tom **10.** Susan

Weather Report (p. 40)

1. c **2.** e **3.** g **4.** d **5.** b **6.** h **7.** i **8.** f **9.** a

Map Views (pp. 45–46)

1. Economic Development **2.** Defense **3.** Tourism **4.** Natural Resources

Unit 4 **Focus**

Job Charts (p. 54)

JOB	PAY	HOURS	PROS	CONS
1. English teacher	$20,000	7:30 AM–4:00 PM	summers off	homework and stress
2. Secretary	$15,000	9:00 AM–5:00 PM	work not difficult; 2 wks. vacation; not a lot of stress	(salary low?)

Continued

Continued

JOB	PAY	HOURS	PROS	CONS
3. Professional baseball player	$600,000	daily practice; spring & baseball seasons	good salary	can't play when older; a lot of stress

What Happened? (pp. 55–56)
The daughter killed her mother by putting a string across the top step of the staircase. The daughter struggled with her mother to make her go down the stairs. The mother then tripped and fell down the stairs.

Matching Paragraphs (p. 57)
paragraph **1:** b paragraph **2:** e paragraph **3:** d
paragraph **4:** c **does not match**: a

Unit 5 Classification

Puzzle Information (p. 73)

Name/Floor	Floor	Married	Saturday Activity
Taiko	above Fatima		
Mai-Li	between Ana & Fatima		
Ana			
Fatima	1 or 3	yes	shopping
1st floor		yes	work
2nd floor		no	
3rd floor		yes	
4th floor		no	

1. Fatima is married and therefore lives on the first or third floor. She shops on Saturdays, but the woman on the first floor works. Fatima lives on the third floor. **2.** Taiko lives above Fatima. She must live on the fourth floor. **3.** The other married person lives on the first floor. We know that Mai-Li lives between Ana and Fatima. Since Fatima lives on the third floor, Ana must live on the first floor. **4.** The remaining person is Mai-Li on the second floor.

Outlines (p. 74)

I. Pets are important to people
    A. Companionship
        1. to older people
        2. to children
    B. Protection
        1. watch dogs
        2. guard snakes
    C. Assistance to the handicapped
        1. guide dogs
        2. hearing dogs
        3. monkeys for paraplegics
II. Pets are important to businesses
    A. Pet food
        1. production
        2. marketing
    B. Other pet products
        1. cages
        2. equipment
    C. Luxuries
        1. sweaters
        2. jeweled collars
    D. Services
        1. haircuts
        2. medical treatment
            a. veterinarians
            b. psychiatrists

Unit 6 Sequence

Next Number (p. 83)
1. c-7 **2.** e-1560 **3.** a-18 **4.** f-36 **5.** b-62 **6.** h-462 **7.** d-89 **8.** g-110

Which Came First? (p. 84)
1. horses, carriages, cars, planes, rockets **2.** washing machines, refrigerators, dishwashers, microwave ovens **3.** sundials, watches, atomic clocks **4.** stone tools, iron tools, bronze tools **5.** phonographs, tape recorders, radios, televisions, VCRs **6.** clubs, bows and arrows, rifles

Chinese Horoscope (pp. 85–86)
p. 85 Ox-1949 Dragon-1940 Sheep-1955
Tiger-1962 Dog-1970 Cock-1969
Boar-1947 Horse-1978 Snake-1977
Monkey-1968 Rat-1972 Rabbit-1963

Continued

Continued

p. 86 Tiger-1986 Rabbit-1987 Dragon-1988 Snake-1989 Horse-1990 Sheep-1991 Monkey-1992 Cock-1993 Dog-1994 Boar-1995 Rat-1996 Ox-1985

What's the Procedure? (p. 88)

Using Chopsticks

1. Hold one chopstick as you would hold a pencil. Press it/the chopstick with your thumb against your/the middle and index fingers. **2.** While still holding the first chopstick, put the second/other chopstick between your middle finger and the base of your thumb. **3.** Keep the chopstick firmly in place with the end of your fourth finger. **4.** Now hold the chopsticks vertically/in an upright position/straight up, tips down, just above your food/plate. **5.** Place the tip of the second chopstick under the food and grasp it firmly.

Using a Pay Phone

1. Find a telephone booth. **2.** Pick up the receiver and insert the necessary coins/money. **3.** Dial the number. **4.** If the line is busy, hang up. **5.** Be sure to check the return slot to get your money back.

Changing a Light Bulb

1. Be sure that the light/lamp is turned OFF. **2.** Remove the old (light) bulb carefully. **3.** Screw/Put in the new light bulb. **4.** Turn it carefully but/and firmly until it is tight. **5.** Turn the light ON.

Unit 7: Cause and Effect

Riddles (p. 95)

1. White. It was a polar bear. Only at the North Pole could you walk equal distances south, east, and north and still return to the same point. **2.** The famous scientist was his sister. **3.** He was walking. **4.** The parrot was deaf. **5.** There were only three people: a grandfather, his son, and his grandson. **6.** An hour and a quarter equals 75 minutes.

Tell Me Why (p. 99)

1. When you hear your voice in normal conversation, much of the sound comes to you through the bones of your head. When you listen to a recording, the sound comes to you through your ears the way people's voices do. A good tape recording gives you an idea of how your voice sounds to other people. **2.** A raw egg is not stable because it is asymmetric. **3.** As the air goes up the mountain, it expands and therefore cools as the atmospheric pressure lessens. **4.** If pie pan bottoms are painted black, they will absorb heat faster. Therefore, pies will heat faster. **5.** Light colored clothing reflects more light than dark clothing does. **6.** Snow is not a good conductor of heat. Consequently, snow acts as an insulator.

Unit 8

Comparison and Contrast

Country X and the U.S. (p. 107)

1. 11 **2.** no match (students must write on) **3.** 8 **4.** no match **5.** 10 **6.** 9 **7.** 12

Matching Proverbs (p. 108–109)

Note: Other answers are possible and should be accepted if students can justify them.

Similar

1. 19 **3.** 15 **4.** 8, 20 **6.** 12 **8.** 14 **10.** 21, 22 **11.** 23 **14.** 23 **16.** 22

Different

1. 7 **2.** 4 **6.** 18 **8.** 11, 23 **12.** 13, 18